C0-DUN-413

DISASTERS

BY

DON BLATTNER AND LISA HOWERTON

COPYRIGHT © 1999 Mark Twain Media, Inc.

ISBN 1–58037–101–9

Printing No. CD–1317

Mark Twain Media, Inc., Publishers
Distributed by Carson-Dellosa Publishing Company, Inc.

The purchase of this book entitles the buyer to reproduce the student pages for classroom use only. Other permissions may be obtained by writing Mark Twain Media, Inc., Publishers.

All rights reserved. Printed in the United States of America.

Table of Contents

Introduction v

Disasters 1
   Disasters 1
   Disasters Crossword Puzzle 2
   Design a Disaster Theme Park 4

Air and Space Disasters 5
   A Giant Falls (The *Hindenburg* Disaster) 5
      Experiments With Static Electricity 7
      St. Elmo's Fire 8
      Sabotage 10
      Hindenburg Disaster Reports 11
   The Death of a Dream (The *Challenger* Explosion) 12
      Launch Your Own Shuttle 14
      NASA vs. the Engineers 16
      Christa McAuliffe's Journal 17
   Terror in the Sky (The Crash of TWA Flight 800) 20
      TWA Flight 800 Quiz 21
      What Do You Think Really Happened? 21

Avalanches and Landslides 22
   Avalanches and Landslides 22
      Avalanche and Landslide Vocabulary 24

Blizzards 25
   Blizzards 25
      Blizzard Vocabulary 26
   White Out (The Blizzard of 1888) 27
      Check Your Knowledge of the Blizzard of 1888 28
      Surviving a Blizzard 29

Chemical and Oil Spills 30
   A Dark and Deadly Shroud (The Valdez Oil Spill) 30
      Experiments With the Way Oil Spreads 32
      Experiments in Cleaning Up Oil Spills 34
      What Went Wrong? 36
   When the Lights Dimmed in the Ukraine (The Chernobyl Disaster) 37
      Chernobyl Vocabulary 38
      Extinguish a Fire 39

Famines, Droughts, and Heat Waves 40
   A Blight Upon the Land (The Irish Potato Famine) 40
      Check Your Knowledge of Ireland and the Famine 42

© Mark Twain Media, Inc., Publishers

Black Blizzard (Dust Bowl Drought of the 1930s) 43
    Research and Thinking for the Dust Bowl 45
    Dust Bowl Vocabulary 46
Improving Your Vocabulary 48

Earthquakes 50
Earthquakes 50
    Famous Earthquakes in History 51
    Earthquake Vocabulary 52
    Identify the Layers of the Earth 53
    Research and Thinking for Earthquakes 54
The Day the Mississippi Ran Backwards (The New Madrid Earthquake of 1811) 55
    Checking What You Have Read—The New Madrid Quake 57
The Day the Earth Danced (San Francisco Quake of 1906) 58
    California and the San Andreas Fault 60
    How Are Earthquakes Measured? 61
    Surviving an Earthquake 62
    Improving Your Vocabulary 63

Fires 65
Risking Death for $9 a Week (The Triangle Shirtwaist Co. Fire) 65
    Research and Thinking for the Triangle Shirtwaist Co. Fire 68

Floods 69
Floods 69
    Flood Vocabulary 70
The Raging Mississippi (De Soto Expedition of 1539, The Flood of 1927,
    The Flood of 1937) 71
    Checking What You Have Read—The Raging Mississippi 73
And a Great Flood Covered the Land (The Mid-America Flood of 1993) 74
    How Well Do You Know the Mississippi? 76
    Famous Rivers 76
Torrents of Destruction (The Johnstown Flood of 1889) 77
    Research and Thinking for the Johnstown Flood 79

Plagues and Epidemics 80
The Horse Was Named Pestilence, and the Rider Was Death (The Black Death) 80
    Black Death Vocabulary 82

Tropical Storms 83
Tropical Storms 83
    Hurricane Vocabulary 84
A Killer Stalks the Resort (The Galveston Hurricane of 1900) 85
    Galveston Learns From the Hurricane 86
Camille Was No Lady (Hurricane Camille of 1969) 87
Andrew Was No Gentleman (Hurricane Andrew of 1992) 88
    Three Infamous U.S. Hurricanes 89

The Worst U.S. Hurricanes of the Twentieth Century 90
    Research and Thinking for Hurricanes 91

Meteorological Hazards **92**
The Day the Earth Shook and the Dinosaurs Died (The Yucatan Asteroid) 92
    Death of the Dinosaurs Vocabulary 94
    Extinction of the Dinosaurs Report 96
    Making a Fossil 97

Maritime Disasters **98**
Death on the Mississippi (The *Sultana* Steamship Explosion of 1865) 98
    Reading a Map 100
    Sultana Study Question 100
    Steamboats and the Mississippi Quiz 101
The Unthinkable Strikes the Unsinkable (The *Titanic* Tragedy of 1912) 103
    Make Your Own Iceberg 105
    You Are the Captain 106
    Different Rules for Different Classes 107

Terrorism **108**
The Oklahoma City Bombing 108
    Oklahoma City Quiz 109
    Research and Thinking on Terrorism 110

Tornadoes **111**
A Swirling Funnel of Death (Tornadoes) 111
    Create Your Own Tornado 112
    Make Tornado Air Rings 112
    Make a Bolt of Lightning 113
    Measure the Speed of Wind 114

Tsunami **115**
Killer Wave (Tsunami) 115
Research and Thinking on Tsunamis 116

Volcanoes **117**
A Sleeping Giant Awakes (The Eruption of Mount Saint Helens) 117
    Volcanoes Vocabulary 118
A Gentle Neighbor Turns Deadly (Mount Vesuvius) 119
    Build Your Own Volcano 120
    Build an Underwater Volcano 121

Possible Future Disasters **122**
Checking What You Have Read 126
Create a Disaster Scenario 128

Answer Key **129**

Introduction

The earth can be a beautiful place. It provides food, shelter, and countless pleasures to humans. It can also be a dangerous place. It can cause death, damage, and complete destruction of hundreds of years of work in a matter of minutes. Even before humans made their appearance, storms, quakes, landslides, meteors, volcanoes, and other forces ripped, tore, and pelted the earth, eliminating many forms of life and causing scars that are apparent even today. Primitive humans, for the most part, were powerless against these sudden and random catastrophic occurrences. They believed these catastrophes were a punishment from God over which they had no control. Today we have a better understanding of the earth and are more able to deal with the natural forces that cause these disasters. While we cannot eliminate most of these violent forces, we are able to predict many of them and, consequently, protect ourselves from them.

In spite of our technology, which enables us to analyze the forces of nature and predict approaching disasters, each year tens of thousands of people are killed by these catastrophic forces. In addition, millions of dollars of property in the form of homes, schools, and commercial buildings are lost. While we strive to eliminate the deaths and minimize the damage caused by these calamities, it is important to note that many of the problems we blame on nature are really our own fault. We know that hurricanes are destructive and occur along our southern coastline, but since we love the beaches and the beautiful weather, we build expensive homes, hotels, and condominiums and settle there. We know the Mississippi River floods periodically, but since we were raised along its banks and the flood plain offers great farm land, we rebuild after a flood. We know of the dangers of an earthquake, but we continue to build and develop along the San Andreas fault along the Pacific coast. Mother Nature may seem ruthless, but without our help, she would not seem nearly so destructive.

The purpose of this book is to describe and explain many of the most catastrophic disasters in history. Because there have been so many disasters, it is impossible to include them all. In fact, many of the worst disasters are not listed in the book. The following criteria were used when deciding which disasters to include:

• *Loss of Life*. Loss of life is a well-known and widely accepted method of defining the importance of a disaster. The bubonic plague, or the black death, as it was called, would have to be included in any book on disasters, since it claimed the lives of one-quarter of Europe's population in the fourteenth century.

• *Historical Significance*. Some events had more of a historical impact than others. An example is the Irish Potato Famine in the 1840s, which not only caused thousands of Irish to emigrate to North America, but also perpetuated a hatred of the English by the Irish. This hatred, which has simmered for over 150 years, is still apparent and the cause of many problems that exist between the countries today.

• *Political Significance*. Closely related to historical significance is political significance. The drought and Dust Bowl in the southern section of the Great Plains in the 1930s had a great deal of political significance. In order to help the farmers in this area, many agricultural programs were begun by the federal government. Not only did the government provide aid, but they also provided advice on how to farm and preserve the land.

• *Location*. It is apparent that students are most affected and should be more aware of those disasters that have occurred in their own country. So the San Francisco Earthquake, which claimed the lives of 850 people, is included in the book, but the earthquake in Shensi China, which occurred in 1556 and claimed almost 10 times as many lives, is not.

• *Date*. Recent disasters have more significance to students, so they are included. For example, the 1993 flood occurring in the Midwest, which caused 50 deaths and left 70,000 homeless, is described, while the flood in China in 1642, which killed 300,000, is not.

• *General Knowledge*. There are some disasters that are so well-known that students just need to be aware of them. The sinking of the S.S. *Titanic* is an excellent example. In terms of loss of life, it certainly would not rank as one of the more significant disasters in history. Yet, of all disasters, it is one that most people know about and are able to discuss.

This book will also point out the positive effects of some disasters. While the human suffering associated with the disaster will be made clear, the legacy or outcome of the disaster can often be positive. A hurricane that kills hundreds of people encourages the city that was hit to erect a sea wall to protect it, and in the future, citizens are more likely to heed hurricane warnings. A drought and soil erosion made worse by poor farming techniques foster improved farming techniques. A plague that ravages an entire continent encourages scholars to become more scientific and less superstitious in their beliefs.

© Mark Twain Media, Inc., Publishers

Disasters

Disasters can be defined as sudden, dangerous occurrences that affect many people and happen without warning. There are two kinds of disasters. First, there is the **natural disaster**, which is caused by nature. Some natural disasters are:

- avalanches and landslides
- earthquakes
- famines, droughts, and heat waves
- floods
- hurricanes
- insect infestations
- meteorological hazards
- storms
- tsunamis
- tornadoes
- volcanoes

Most natural disasters are unavoidable. For example, there is little we can do to stop a tornado. The most we can do is to take cover and hope we survive. The same can be said for most other natural disasters. Humans, for the most part, are powerless to stop them. We are, however, becoming more successful at predicting natural disasters so that we can avoid them. Our success in being able to identify conditions that might cause a disaster, however, has its problems. If people are constantly warned that conditions which might cause a tornado exist and none occurs, they may begin to ignore the warnings.

Another kind of disaster is the kind of disaster caused by humans. These are often called **man-made disasters**. Some man-made disasters are:

- air and space disasters
- chemical and oil spills
- explosions
- fires
- hysteria
- rail disasters
- sailing disasters
- terrorism

Sometimes it is difficult to put disasters into these two categories. Explosions and fires, for example, are usually classified as man-made disasters. But, we know that when a volcano erupts, there is a loud explosion and the advancing lava burns everything in its path. On the other hand, humans can contribute to natural disasters. Poor land management by farmers can lead to insect infestations, soil erosion, and eventually famine.

© Mark Twain Media, Inc., Publishers

Name _____ Date _____

Disasters Crossword Puzzle

How familiar are you with various disasters? This puzzle will check your knowledge. Use the clues on page 3 to complete the puzzle below.

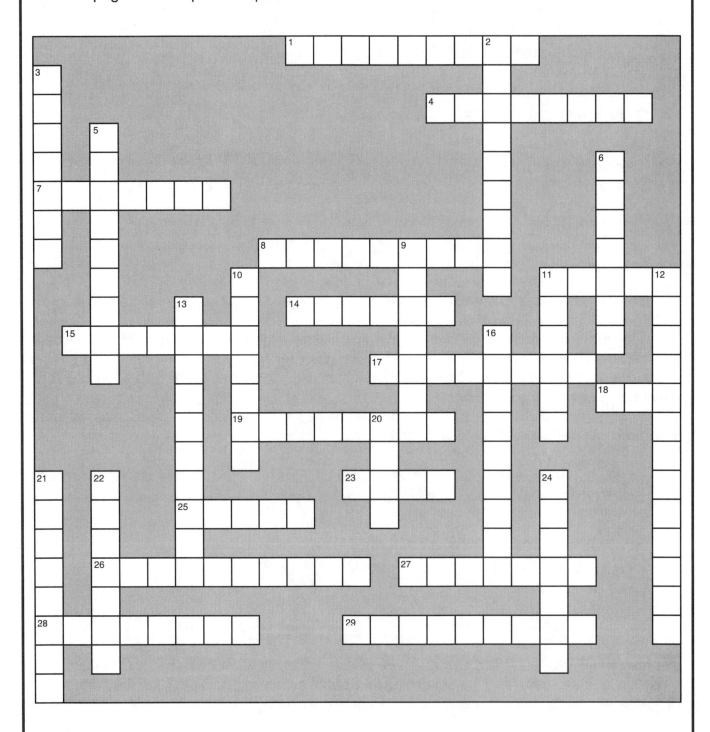

Name_____ Date _____

Disasters Crossword Puzzle Clues

Use the clues below to complete the puzzle on page 2.

ACROSS

1. Generally refers to a mass of snow falling down a mountainside

4. A disaster involving a ship or boat is called a _____ disaster.

7. A tropical cyclone that occurs in the western Pacific or Indian oceans

8. Contamination of soil, water, or air

11. An excess of water in an area that is usually dry

14. An infectious epidemic disease

15. The eruption of molten material and gases from the earth's surface

17. Microorganisms that sometimes cause disease

18. Disasters occurring during flight are called _____ disasters.

19. Uncontrolled emotions

23. A flame or conflagration

25. A layer of gas that surrounds the earth and protects against the ultraviolet rays of the Sun

26. The sudden movement of the earth's crust

27. Scientists worry that global _____ will cause more heat waves and droughts.

28. A small celestial body that sometimes strikes the earth

29. The downhill movement of a mass of soil, mud, or rocks

DOWN

2. A severe storm of swirling winds of more than 75 m.p.h.

3. A slang term for a tornado

5. A sudden, violent release of energy, sometimes caused by a bomb

6. Another name for a hurricane

9. A giant wave

10. A long period without rain

11. Shortage of food for a long period

12. The destruction of forests

13. A tornado over water

16. Violence by a person or organized group against another

20. A disaster involving a train is called a____ disaster.

21. A heavy snowstorm with strong winds and cold temperatures

22. Small creatures that sometimes devour crops, causing a famine

24. A funnel-shaped storm on land that may travel as fast as 200 m.p.h. or more

© Mark Twain Media, Inc., Publishers

Name _____ Date _____

Design a Disaster Theme Park

You probably have attended a theme park at some time. Theme parks are fun and entertaining, but have you ever considered how they are designed? What kind of thought and planning goes into the rides, entertainment, foods, refreshments, and souvenirs? Is the layout random, or is the design based on an overall plan? Here is your chance to show how creative you are by helping to design a theme park. The teacher may decide to make an assignment for the entire class or break the class into several groups and have each group develop its own theme park.

If the teacher decides on several different groups, four or five students will be assigned to each group. Each group has the responsibility of designing a theme park. The general theme for the park is disasters. Everything in the park should reflect the theme.

Here are the steps each group will go through to complete the assignment.
1. Discuss theme parks each member has attended.
2. Decide who your customers will be. What are they like? How old are they?
3. Decide where your theme park should be located.
4. Based on your discussion, make a list of the rides, shows, activities, entertainment, and food you would like to include in your theme park. Remember to tie your theme into as much of the park as you can.
5. List the specific jobs that need to be completed. Here is a partial list of those jobs. Your group will probably think of others.
   • Design several rides. Name them and explain how they work. Remember, be sure to include different kinds of rides and rides for different age groups. All of the rides must relate to the disaster theme.
   • Decide what theme-related activities you might have in your park.
   • Decide what other theme-related entertainment you might have in your park.
   • Decide on the number, kinds, and names of the restaurants in your park. Make out a complete menu for one of the restaurants. Be sure to give your food special theme-related names. Using a computer, create the menu to be displayed in class.
   • Decide what kinds of gifts you will sell in the souvenir shops.
   • Decide what kinds of workers you will need for your theme park and how they should be dressed.
   • Create a layout or map for the theme park showing where everything is located.
6. The jobs should then be divided up so that each person in the group has the same amount of work to do. You might decide that one person should create all of the rides and that another should create all of the activities or entertainment. Or you might decide that each person in the group should create one ride, one entertainment, one activity, and so on.
7. After all of the assignments are complete, each person should make a report back to his or her group.
8. The groups can discuss each report, make changes if desired, and put the report on a computer so that copies can be printed for other class members.
9. Each group should present its theme park to the class. One person will present the plan, but all in the group will be available to answer questions or explain the specific parts of the park they developed. Copies of all of the materials, including the map, should be made available to class members.

A Giant Falls

The *Hindenburg* Disaster

The *Hindenburg* was a grand airship known as a **dirigible**, a word derived from a Latin word that means "to steer" or "to direct." It was also sometimes called a **zeppelin** after Count Ferdinand von Zeppelin, a master of airship design. It was built in 1936 by Luftshiffbau Zeppelin, a German company that had already built nearly 120 airships.

In 1933, Adolf Hitler and the Nazi party had risen to power in Germany. Soon after becoming the dictator of Germany, Hitler insisted on having a swastika, the Nazi symbol, displayed on all ships and aircraft made in the country. The *Hindenburg* was no exception. A silver-coated gray fabric stretched over the entire metal frame of the airship, with swastikas proudly painted on its tailfins.

The *Hindenburg* was the largest airship of its kind ever built. Measuring 803.8 feet long, the cigar-shaped craft was the length of three football fields. It had a diameter of 135 feet and required seven million cubic feet of hydrogen gas (an invisible, flammable gas) to fill its 16 airtight compartments.

The airship was powered by propellers that were turned by four diesel engines, giving the ship a top speed of 60 to 80 miles per hour. This enabled passengers to be ferried across the Atlantic Ocean in a mere 60 hours. Previously, travelers could only cross the vast ocean by way of boat, taking approximately four weeks to reach their destination. Compared with the four days it took the *Hindenburg* to make the journey, it is easy to see why the airship was a popular choice of transportation for the 12 months that it was in service.

With prices ranging from $400 to $680 for a one-way ticket and $720 to $1,224 for a round-trip ticket, a ride on the mighty ship could only be afforded by the very wealthy. However, many felt the price was well worth it. To ride on the *Hindenburg* was to travel in the height of luxury. It was often compared to staying in a five-star hotel in the air.

Accommodations on the ship included 25 passenger cabins, shower rooms, a kitchen, a dining room, a dance floor with a stage for a band, lounges with observation decks, and, amazingly, a smoking room.

As you can imagine, in a ship filled with highly flammable gas, great precautions had to be taken in the smoking room. As the passengers boarded the *Hindenburg*, all matches and lighters were taken from them. In the smoking room, there was only one cigarette lighter, an electric, and it was chained to the wall. In addition, the hallways and ladders were coated

> **Disaster at a Glance**
> **What:** A dirigible, the *Hindenburg*, burns and crashes
> **Where:** Lakehurst, New Jersey
> **When:** May 6, 1937
> **Deaths:** 36
> **Aftermath:** The popularity of dirigibles stopped abruptly. The cause of the fire was never discovered.

with rubber in order to reduce the threat of static electricity. Many of the passengers did feel safe enough to smoke in this designated area.

Because of precautions such as these, the German zeppelins boasted a remarkable safety record. In fact, the *Hindenburg* and her sister ships had crossed the Atlantic hundreds of times without a single mishap.

However, all this came to an abrupt halt on May 6, 1937. As the *Hindenburg* began to land in Lakehurst, New Jersey, the ship suddenly burst into flames. On the ground was Herbert Morrison, a radio reporter for WLS in Chicago. He began what he thought was to be a routine broadcast, but it became a newscast that made history.

"Well, here it comes, ladies and gentlemen, and what a sight it is, a thrilling one, a marvelous sight…It's practically standing still now. They've dropped ropes out of the nose of the ship, and they've been taken ahold of on the field by a number of men. The vast motors of the ship are just holding it, just enough to keep it from…"

Then there was a two-second pause.

"Oh, oh, oh!…It's burst into flames!" Morrison shouted. "Get out of the way, please, oh, my, this is terrible, oh my, get out of the way, please! It is burning, bursting into flames and is falling … Oh! This is one of the worst…Oh! It's a terrific sight…Oh! It's crashing…bursting into flames, and it's falling on the mooring mast and all the folks between us. This is terrible," Morrison said sobbing. "This is one of the worst catastrophes in the world."

"This is terrible…Oh, the humanity and all the passengers…a mass of flaming wreckage. Honestly, I can hardly breathe…I'm going to step inside where I can't see it…It's terrible…I…Folks, I'm going to have to stop for a moment, because I've lost my voice. This is the worst thing I've ever witnessed."

A motion-picture cameraman was standing nearby filming the ground crew at the time of the explosion. He suddenly felt a horrible blast of heat, and his assistant shouted, "Point the camera up!" The cameraman quickly focused his camera on the *Hindenburg,* which was now engulfed in flames and crashing quickly. He was able to capture the entire scene, all the while repeating, "Oh, my God! Oh, my God!"

Throughout the crash, heroism reigned. United States Navy Chief Fred "Bull" Tobin was in charge of the ground crew that day. When he saw the *Hindenburg* burst into flames, he commanded his crew, "Stand fast, men. We have to help those people inside." The ground crew, following his command, risked their own lives to help save the passengers.

The ordeal lasted exactly 34 seconds. When it was over, all that remained of the mighty ship was the metal framework. Remarkably, with 97 people aboard the ship that day, only 36 people perished—22 crew members, 13 passengers, and one man on the ground.

Contrary to popular belief, Morrison's coverage of the disaster was not broadcast live. He and an engineer had been experimenting with field recordings that day, and it was not until the next day that people across the country heard the tragic broadcast. In fact, it was the first recorded radio news report to be nationally broadcast by NBC.

Soon after, this news report was added to the film footage taken that day and shown in newsreels in theaters across the country. This was the first disaster of great magnitude that had been captured on film, and it made a huge impact on the nation of viewers. As a result, travelers lost their faith in the safety of the airships, and their use for travel ended as abruptly as the last flight of the *Hindenburg.* And, although many theories still circulate, a definite cause for the explosion of the *Hindenburg* was never found.

Name _____ Date _____

Experiments With Static Electricity

One of the more popular theories explaining the *Hindenburg* explosion was the presence of static electricity. There had been a thunderstorm in Lakehurst earlier that day. Supporters of the theory believe the cables that were dropped to the ground during landing served as a conductor. This conductor created a spark, which in turn ignited the free-floating hydrogen. Here is an experiment that will enable you to understand static electricity better.

What You'll Need:

- A balloon
- A flat baking tray
- A glass
- A wool sweater

Follow these steps.

1. Place the baking tray on top of the glass.
2. Rub the balloon on the sweater for several seconds.
3. Place the balloon on top of the tray.
4. Now, put your finger close to, but not touching, the edge of the tray.

Answer the following questions.

1. What happens?

_____

_____

_____

_____

2. Why do you suppose this occurred?

_____

_____

_____

_____

© Mark Twain Media, Inc., Publishers

Name_____ Date _____

3. What do you think of the popular theory that static electricity caused the explosion of the *Hindenburg?*

_____

_____

_____

_____

4. How do you think a theory such as this could be investigated in order to prove or disprove it?

_____

_____

_____

_____

5. How could this have caused the *Hindenburg* disaster?

_____

_____

_____

_____

_____

_____

_____

_____

_____

_____

Name _____ Date _____

St. Elmo's Fire

Another theory cited by investigators claimed the phenomenon known as "St. Elmo's Fire" caused the *Hindenburg* disaster.

1. Using sources found at your local library and on the Internet, explain what St. Elmo's Fire is in your own words.

_____

_____

_____

_____

_____

2. What do you think of this theory?

_____

_____

_____

_____

3. How do you think a theory such as this could be investigated in order to prove or disprove it?

_____

_____

_____

_____

_____

_____

_____

_____

_____

Name _____ Date _____

Sabotage

Another theory to explain the *Hindenburg* disaster was sabotage. Although many people believed this to be true, Adolf Hitler tried to suppress this theory from circulating in Germany. In fact, anyone in Germany caught discussing the possibility of the *Hindenburg* being sabotaged was severely punished.

1. Why do you suppose this was? _____

_____

_____

2. Why would someone want to sabotage the *Hindenburg?* _____

_____

_____

3. Who may have done it? _____

_____

4. What methods could they have used? _____

_____

_____

5. What do you think of this theory? _____

_____

_____

6. How do you think a theory such as this could be investigated in order to prove or disprove it?

_____

_____

_____

_____

_____

Name _____ Date _____

Hindenburg Disaster Reports

Divide students into several groups. Each group will be assigned one theory explaining why the *Hindenburg* caught fire and crashed. There does not have to be a group for each theory, but there should be at least three different groups. Some of the theories to be considered are that the *Hindenburg* crash was caused by:

- static electricity.
- St. Elmo's Fire.
- sabotage.
- other theories the students might develop.

Follow these steps to complete the assignment.

1. As a group, students will gather information and develop arguments to support their theory.
2. The group will write a report explaining their theory and provide reasons why they believe it is the most logical explanation for the *Hindenburg* tragedy. The report will include the following information:
    - An introduction stating the question they are trying to answer and various theories that have been presented to answer the question.
    - An explanation of the theory they support.
    - Arguments to support the theory.
    - Arguments that criticize other theories.
    - Any other relative information.
    - A conclusion.
3. After the reports are finished, each group will have an opportunity to orally present its paper to the class.
4. Each member of the group will be expected to participate in the presentation; perhaps each person will present one portion of the paper.
5. After the presentation, the class will question the group's findings and debate the theory.
6. The process will be repeated for each group.
7. The papers may then be combined on the computer and printed as a book entitled, *The Hindenburg: A Study of the Theories Surrounding the Disaster.* The class can decide if their book should stress one theory over another.
8. Copies of the book should be kept in the classroom for future classes and presented to the school library.

The Death of a Dream

THE *CHALLENGER* EXPLOSION

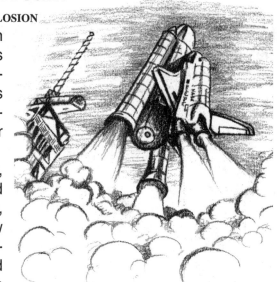

Challenger Flight 51-L was the first shuttle mission in history to carry two civilians on board. One was Charles Jarvis, one of two engineers from Hughes Aircraft Company chosen to ride in the shuttle. Jarvis was an obvious choice because he was the manager in charge of designing the Leasat satellites, which used the shuttle as their primary launch vehicle.

The second civilian on board was Christa McAuliffe, winner of President Ronald Reagan's newly established Teacher in Space program. McAuliffe taught economics, law, and American history at Concord High School in New Hampshire. She was married and had two young children. The fact that she was an "all-American girl" seemed to spark the nation's interest. Americans once again began to show interest in the space program—interest that had not been there for over 10 years.

Besides Jarvis and McAuliffe, there were five other astronauts scheduled to ride on the shuttle that day. They included Francis R. Scobee, the mission commander; Mike Smith, the pilot; Judith Resnik, who would be in charge of operating the remote manipulator arm; physicist Ronald McNair, who would be observing Halley's Comet; and Ellison Onizuka, who would be in charge of deploying the TDRS-B satellite.

Even with all the preparations being made and the positive publicity surrounding the shuttle, *Challenger* Flight 51-L seemed to be cursed from the very beginning. It was originally scheduled to be launched in December of 1985. However, unforeseen delays made launching on this date impossible. The launch was then rescheduled for Friday, January 24, 1986. Then, Friday afternoon, it was announced that the flight would be delayed until Monday, January 27.

Early Monday morning, the crew boarded the shuttle and were strapped into position. But, at nine minutes prior to takeoff, a mechanic found a faulty bolt on one of the doors. The launch was stopped until the necessary repairs could be made.

It was not until four hours later that it was announced the door was finally repaired. But, by then, the wind had begun blowing much too hard, and the launch had to be delayed yet again. This time it was rescheduled for Tuesday, January 28.

Monday afternoon, temperatures began to drop drastically, and there were reports of freezing temperatures. Several engineers advised that the launch be delayed until more favorable conditions existed. They believed such cold temperatures would have an adverse effect on the solid rocket boosters' O-rings. However, these warnings were ignored by NASA officials. They thought the launch had been delayed too many times already.

Tuesday morning, spectators began to arrive at Cape Canaveral. Among the interested viewers were many of the shuttle crew's family and friends. They watched the *Challenger* expectantly as the countdown began over the loudspeaker. When "lift-off!" was finally announced, cheers and screams of delight could be heard throughout the bleachers.

Flight control and communication with the crew was then immediately switched to Mission Control in Houston.

DISASTER AT A GLANCE

WHAT: A United States space shuttle explodes

WHERE: Cape Canaveral, Florida

WHEN: January 28, 1986

AFTERMATH: NASA re-evaluated the shuttle program, mapping out specific goals. It made several safety improvements.

© Mark Twain Media, Inc., Publishers

Over the loudspeakers, the audience listened to the exchange between the *Challenger* crew and Mission Control.

T plus 0:07—Mission Control: Watch your roll, *Challenger.*

Scobee: Houston, *Challenger* roll program. (This is the first maneuver that is done after lift-off. It rotates the shuttle so that it is facing the earth.)

Mission Control: Roll program confirmed. *Challenger* now heading down range. Engines beginning to throttle down to 94 percent…Will throttle down to 65 percent shortly. Velocity 2,257 feet per second (1,538 miles per hour). Altitude 4.3 nautical miles. Three engines running normally … Engines throttling up. Three engines now at 104 percent.

T plus 0:11—Smith: Go,…!

T plus 0:19—Smith: Looks like we've got a lot of wind up here today.

T plus 0:21—Scobee: Yeah. It's a little hard to see out my window here.

T plus 0:28—Smith: There's 10,000 feet and Mach point five (This is half the speed of sound).

T plus 0:35—Scobee: Point nine.

T plus 0:40—Smith: There's Mach 1.

T plus 0:41—Scobee: Going through 19,000 feet.

T plus 0:43—Scobee: Okay, we're throttling down.

T plus 0:57—Scobee: Throttling up.

T plus 0:58—Smith: Throttle up.

T plus 0:59—Scobee: Roger.

T plus 1:02—Smith: Thirty-five thousand. Going through 1.5.

T plus 1:05—Scobee: Reading 486 on mine (airspeed indicator).

T plus 1:07—Smith: Yep. That's what I've got, too.

Mission Control: Go at throttle up.

T plus 1:10—Scobee: Roger, go at throttle up.

T plus 1:13—Smith: Uhh…oh!

Then, all communication between Mission Control and the shuttle ceased. A little over a minute passed as the audience continued to watch the ascent of the shuttle. Then, disbelief swept the crowd as the shuttle burst into flames.

No sound came from the loudspeakers for about 30 seconds. Finally, Mission Control announced: "Flight controllers are looking very carefully at the situation. Obviously a major malfunction. We have no downwind. We have a report from the flight dynamics officer that the vehicle has exploded. The flight director confirms that. We are looking at all contingency operations, waiting for word of any recovery forces in the down-range field."

None of the crew survived the blast. The *Challenger* did not have a launch escape system, so even if the crew did have a chance at survival, they would still have been trapped inside. Even with an escape system, it is not likely that anyone would have survived such a horrendous disaster for long.

In the end, inspectors ruled that the cause of the explosion was the failure of the O-ring pressure seals. It was simply too cold for the seals to work properly—exactly what NASA had been warned of the previous night.

As a result of the shuttle explosion, NASA was forced to re-examine the role of the shuttle in its space program. It mapped out certain goals for the shuttle, the primary goal being the transport of people and supplies needed to construct space stations. NASA also made sure the shuttle was a safer vehicle. Several safety improvements were made—most notably, the addition of an escape system for the crew.

Name _____ Date _____

Launch Your Own Shuttle

What You'll Need:

- Two $8\frac{1}{2}$ x 12-inch pieces of paper
- A cardboard tube about $\frac{3}{4}$-inch in diameter
- Cellophane tape

1. Wrap one of the pieces of paper around the tube and tape the edges together. The paper should form a tube around the cardboard tube and should be loose enough to move freely up and down.
2. Remove the paper tube from around the cardboard tube.
3. Flatten one end of the paper tube, fold it over, and seal it with tape.
4. Take the other sheet of paper and carefully fold it in half lengthwise.
5. Following the diagram, make the final four folds. This will form the shape of your shuttle.

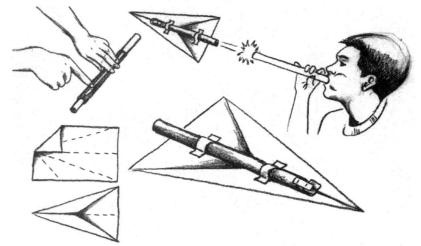

6. Tape the paper tube down the center of your shuttle as shown.
7. Attach the cardboard tube to the open end of the paper tube on your shuttle.
8. In an open area, put the other end of the cardboard tube in your mouth and blow as hard as you can. This is how you will launch your shuttle.

 A shuttle is different from an ordinary rocket in that it is reusable. The Space Shuttle consists of four major parts: the orbiter, a large external tank, and two solid rocket boosters, or SRBs. Of the four parts, only the external tank cannot be reused. Although your shuttle will not contain four parts, it will, like the real Shuttle, need to remain aerodynamically correct. This means that the design of the body and wings offer the least resistance to the air as it travels to its destination. The more aerodynamically correct your shuttle is, the faster it will travel. Try experimenting with different shapes and sizes when constructing your shuttle and see what effects they have.

Answer the following questions.

1. When you change shuttle designs, is the speed affected?

_____

Name _____ Date _____

2. Why do you suppose this is?

_____

_____

_____

_____

3. Is the flight path affected?

_____

4. Why do you suppose this is?

_____

_____

_____

5. Are you able to construct your shuttle in such a way that it will glide smoothly through the air and to the ground?

_____

6. How were you able to achieve this?

_____

_____

_____

_____

_____

_____

_____

_____

Name _____ Date _____

NASA vs. the Engineers

Prior to the *Challenger* launch, a group of engineers informed NASA of the dangers of launching in freezing temperatures.

1. Do you think they did everything they could to stop the launch?

_____

2. Why or why not?

_____

_____

_____

_____

Now, using sources found at your local library or on the Internet, research the specific problems with the shuttle that day. Imagine you are one of the engineers that advised NASA against launching the space shuttle that day.

3. What would you have done differently?

_____

_____

_____

_____

4. How do you think you could have convinced NASA of the danger?

_____

_____

_____

_____

5. Do you think you could have saved the lives of the crew that day?

_____

_____

Name _____ Date _____

Christa McAuliffe's Journal

Christa McAuliffe was a great believer in keeping a daily journal. She believed that the social history of the United States was passed on by studying journals kept by people during key points in history. As a result, she kept a journal of her own and required her students to do the same. When she was chosen for the Teacher in Space program, she decided to keep a daily journal of her space travel in order to "humanize the Space Age by giving the perspective of a non-astronaut. I think the students will look at that and see that an ordinary person is contributing to history. If they can make that connection, they are going to get excited about history and about the future."

Imagine you are Christa McAuliffe going into space for the first time. Using sources found at your local library and on the Internet, research Christa McAuliffe and NASA's space training program. Now, write a journal describing your days leading up to the shuttle launch. Use the following questions as guidelines in constructing your journal.

1. How did you feel when you were told you won the Teacher in Space contest? _____

_____

_____

_____

2. How do you feel about being the first private citizen in space? _____

_____

_____

3. Are you frightened? Excited? _____

_____

_____

4. How do your family and friends feel about it? _____

_____

_____

5. What does your training consist of? _____

_____

_____

_____

Name _____ Date _____

6. Is it difficult? _____

_____

_____

7. What will your responsibilities be once you board the shuttle? _____

_____

_____

_____

8. How do you feel about your fellow astronauts? _____

_____

_____

9. How do you think they feel about you, a civilian, riding on the shuttle with them? _____

_____

_____

10. How do you feel about the shuttle's delays? _____

_____

_____

11. Do the delays make you nervous or do you still have faith in the shuttle's abilities? _____

_____

_____

12. What were your thoughts while sitting in the shuttle for four hours, waiting for the door to be repaired?

_____

_____

_____

Name_____ Date _____

13. What did you and the other crew members talk about?_____

_____

_____

_____

14. How did you feel when you were told there was yet another delay? _____

_____

_____

15. How do you feel boarding the shuttle? _____

_____

_____

_____

16. Are you nervous? Proud? _____

_____

_____

17. How do you feel at lift-off? _____

_____

_____

_____

18. How do you think your family and friends feel? _____

_____

_____

_____

_____

Terror in the Sky
THE CRASH OF TWA FLIGHT 800

TWA Flight 800, a Boeing 747 jetliner bound for Paris, exploded and crashed into the Atlantic Ocean on July 17, 1996, killing all 230 people on board. The crash occurred 20 miles southeast of East Moriches, a town located on the south shore of Long Island, New York. Among the passengers on board that night were 16 members of a high school French Club from Montoursville, Pennsylvania, who, along with five chaperons, were on their way to Paris, France.

At 8:19 that evening, the flight had taken off from John F. Kennedy Airport. But, by the time it had reached 13,700 feet, at 8:48 p.m., it had disappeared from radar screens. Soon after the crash, the U.S. Coast Guard, aided by local volunteers, including fishermen and boaters, began rescue efforts, but no survivors were found.

The next day, TWA officials reported that the plane had never experienced major mechanical problems, and the crew had not reported any problems to air traffic controllers prior to the crash.

Initially, investigators entertained three possible crash scenarios: a terrorist bomb, a missile launched from the ground, and a mechanical failure. Officials immediately began a massive effort to recover the bodies of the victims and pieces of the wreckage to discover the cause of the crash. Once most of the plane had been recovered, officials began reassembling the plane in a hangar in Calverton, in Long Island, New York. Many pieces were also sent to the FBI's laboratory in Washington, D.C., for analysis.

Witnesses to the crash described seeing an explosion in the sky just prior to the crash, and then a bright red fireball, which, trailing smoke, fell into the ocean. They also said that, after the explosion, the plane seemed to break in two. This stirred speculation the crash was caused by a bomb planted by terrorists. A short, loud sound that was captured on the cockpit voice recorder reinforced this theory. However, neither TWA nor Kennedy Airport had received any terrorist threats prior to the crash. Tests done on crash debris failed to offer conclusive evidence of the presence of explosive residue.

Some witnesses also reported seeing a streak of light heading toward the 747 just prior to the crash. This, coupled with reports of an unexplained blip appearing on radar screens just prior to the crash, fueled rumors that Flight 800 had been hit by a missile. Claims that a U.S. Navy ship had been conducting training exercises near the crash site and accidentally shot down the 747 were quickly dismissed by government officials. These officials cited the fact the plane was flying much too high to be in the range of most surface-to-air missiles.

Fortunately, flight investigators did not need to rely only on witnesses to determine what went wrong with the plane. All commercial planes are equipped with two devices called "black boxes" that give information about the flight. The first device is the **flight data recorder**, which is hooked up to several sensors installed in different areas of the plane. These sensors measure altitude, speed, time, and the positions of the wings and rudders, as well as other important data. The other device is the **cockpit voice recorder** that records the voices of the pilot, copilot, and other crew members. These devices are ruggedly built and well-protected so they will survive a crash.

The National Transportation Safety Board (NTSB) conducted a 16-month investigation, reviewing all of the data available concerning the crash. They concluded that the explosion was most likely due to an ignition of fuel vapors in the jet's central fuel tank.

> **DISASTER AT A GLANCE**
> **WHAT:** A Boeing 747 Jetliner explodes and crashes
> **WHERE:** Just offshore from Long Island, New York
> **WHEN:** July 17, 1996
> **WHY:** Most likely due to an ignition of fuel vapors in the jet's central fuel tank
> **DEATHS:** 230
> **AFTERMATH:** The NTSB asked the FAA to take steps to make fuel tanks in all 747s safer.

© Mark Twain Media, Inc., Publishers

Name_____ Date _____

TWA Flight 800 Quiz

1. The destination of TWA Flight 800 was _____.

2. It exploded and crashed into the _____.

3. The crash killed all _____ people on board.

4. East Moriches is a town located on the south shore of_____, New York.

5. Among the passengers on board that night were 16 members of a high school_____
   Club.

6. The flight had taken off from_____ Airport.

7. Investigators reviewed _____ possible crash scenarios.

8. Officials reassembled the plane in a hangar in_____, in Long Island, New York.

9. Many pieces of the plane were sent to the _____ laboratory in Washington, D.C.,
   for analysis.

10. Witnesses said they saw an explosion in the _____ prior to the crash.

11. A short, loud sound was captured on the_____ voice recorder.

12. Some witnesses also reported seeing a _____ heading to-
    ward the 747 just prior to the crash.

13. Officials claim the plane was flying much too _____ to be in the range of most surface-
    to-air missiles.

14. After a _____ long investigation, the National Transportation Safety Board
    concluded that the explosion was most likely due to an ignition of fuel vapors in the jet's central
    fuel tank.

What Do You Think Really Happened?

Initially, investigators entertained three possible crash scenarios: a terrorist bomb, a missile launched from the ground, and a mechanical failure, before finally ruling the crash a result of mechanical failure. Using sources found at your local library and on the Internet, research these three scenarios or possibly one of your own. Then, write a paper describing what you think really happened that night and why.

© Mark Twain Media, Inc., Publishers   21

Avalanches and Landslides

Like a **tsunami**, an **avalanche** or **landslide** often strikes without warning. Massive amounts of snow, rocks, mud, and debris charge down a mountain or slope at a high speed, crushing everything in its path. An avalanche can destroy an entire town and everyone in it as it rampages down the mountain. The terms *avalanche* and *landslide* are sometimes used interchangeably, as if they are synonyms. Although the terms are similar, most people use the word *avalanche* to refer to snow moving down a hill, mountain, or slope and the word *landslide* to refer to earth, mud, rocks, and **debris** moving down a hill, mountain, or slope.

Every state in the United States has experienced some type of avalanche or landslide, but they are most common in Alaska, Hawaii, the **Appalachian Mountains**, and the **Rocky Mountains**. While avalanches or landslides occur in almost every state in the United States, they are more destructive in other countries. Avalanches and landslides cause between 25 and 50 deaths a year and $1 billion in damages in the United States. Throughout the world, though, hundreds of people die each year, and the cost of damages from these disasters is set in the hundreds of billions of dollars.

AVALANCHES

The biggest avalanches occur in the **Himalayas**, but the avalanches that cause the most deaths occur in the populated valleys of the **Alps**. The European Alps spread over several countries. It is a picturesque area famous for skiing and other winter sports and easily the most densely populated mountain region in the world. What makes this area so vulnerable to avalanches is not only the huge amount of snow it receives each year and the steep mountains unable to hold the snow, but also warm dry winds blow through the valleys, raising the temperatures and melting the snow quickly. The melted snow **seeps** down to the surface of the mountain, loosening the snow and acting as a lubricant between the snow and the mountain. Since the hills and plains of the Alps are fairly smooth, the snow is able to gain tremendous speed and power as it slides and crashes down to the valley below.

Although most deaths from avalanches occur in the Alps, the greatest avalanche occurred in Peru on January 10, 1962. The avalanche that happened on Huascaran, an extinct **volcano** in the **Andes**, destroyed eight villages and killed between 3,000 and 3,500 people. The avalanche traveled 10 miles in seven minutes and grew to a height of over 80 feet before it came to rest.

There are basically four kinds of avalanches.

- **Slab avalanche**. This happens when a large hunk or block of snow breaks loose and slides down a hill.
- **Wet snow avalanche**. These usually occur in the spring. The wet snow becomes a huge ball as it travels down the hill.
- **Dry snow avalanche**. This type of avalanche takes place after a heavy snow fall. The dry snow slides along the ground.
- **Airborne powder avalanche**. Sometimes a dry snow avalanche turns into an airborne powder avalanche. The dry snow rises off the ground as it travels down the hill, becoming a swirling mass hundreds of feet high.

© Mark Twain Media, Inc., Publishers

People who live in avalanche prone areas have taken measures to prevent them from damaging their property or causing deaths. Sometimes, they purposely start small avalanches so that the snow will not build up and cause a large avalanche. They do this by using explosives. They fire mortar shells into the snow, and a small, harmless avalanche comes down the mountain. Another way to protect a home or a village is to erect some type of barrier to stop the snow if an avalanche occurs. They may plant rows of trees between the mountain and the village. Or, they may build a wedge-shaped wall between the mountain and the village. An avalanche that hits the wall will separate and go around the town. Sometimes snow fences are placed higher up on the mountain in order to prevent small avalanches from growing into large ones.

As the popularity of skiing grows, new **resorts**, hotels, restaurants, and other businesses open in the areas most vulnerable to avalanches. This increased development means a growth in population as well as a growth in the tourist industry. In spite of all the efforts to prevent avalanches or to minimize their violence, it is likely that development in these dangerous areas will be followed by an increase of fatalities and property damage as a result of avalanches.

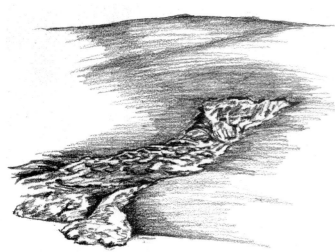

LANDSLIDES

Closely related to avalanches are landslides. Landslide is the term used to describe earth, mud, rocks, or debris moving down a hill, mountain, or slope. Water and **gravity** are the two main causes of landslides. The earth becomes **saturated** after heavy rains or melting snow **penetrates** the top layer of earth and makes the layers underneath slippery. The top layer, heavy because of the saturated soil, breaks away and slides down the mountain. In addition to water and gravity, other circumstances sometimes help cause a landslide. The slope may be weakened by **erosion** or man-made structures. **Vibrations** from **earthquakes**, volcanic activity, machinery, traffic, or **blasting** may create stresses that make weak slopes fail.

There are basically four different kinds of landslides.

- **Rockslides.** When huge chunks of rock break away from the slope, they often slide down the mountain. This sometimes happens if the slope has been cleared of trees and other vegetation that may have held the earth into place before.
- **Rockfalls.** When rocks crash down a mountain or slope, they often knock other rocks or debris loose, which also ricochet off the side of the slope.
- **Flows.** Flows or **mudflows** are wet landslides. They occur after heavy rains.
- **Slumps.** Sometimes the material doesn't really slide down a mountain, but merely "slumps." This happens on steep slopes, and the cliff may tilt backward and collapse or drop toward the slope. The cliff may resemble a series of **terraces** if it slumps.

One of the most devastating landslides occurred in 1970 in the Andes mountains. A mudflow slid down the mountain and 18,000 people were killed. It is estimated that the mudflow created a wave of mud and debris over 260 feet high and moved so fast that it was impossible to escape. It completely destroyed the town of Ungay.

© Mark Twain Media, Inc., Publishers

Name _____ Date _____

Avalanche and Landslide Vocabulary

How well do you understand the following terms dealing with avalanches and landslides? Below and to the left are a number of definitions. In the blank after each definition, write the word that is described by the definition. Use the terms given below.

Definition	**Term**
1. A block of earth tilts back and falls	_____
2. Enters	_____
3. An opening in the earth that emit gases and hot rock	_____
4. A flat, narrow stretch of ground with a steep slope	_____
5. Snow that slides down a slope	_____
6. Wet snow becomes a huge ball as it travels down the hill.	_____
7. When rocks crash down a mountain or slope	_____
8. When huge chunks of rock slide down the mountain	_____
9. The attraction of two masses	_____
10. A mountain system in South America	_____
11. Europe's most expansive mountain system.	_____
12. Giant wave	_____
13. Rock and soil that moves down a slope	_____
14. A rapid motion	_____
15. The wearing away of the earth's surface	_____
16. Completely soaked	_____
17. A huge mass of snow that slides down a slope	_____
18. The most expansive mountain system in North America	_____
19. Dry snow slides along the ground as it goes downhill.	_____
20. Wet landslides	_____
21. A mountain system found in Asia	_____
22. A lodging noted for relaxation or recreation	_____
23. An explosion	_____
24. The dry snow rises off the ground as it travels down the hill.	_____
25. To ooze	_____
26. A mountain system in the eastern United States	_____
27. A violent shaking of the earth's crust	_____
28. Fragments of items; litter, or rubble	_____

airborne powder avalanche, Andes, Alps, Appalachian Mountains, avalanche, blasting, debris, dry snow avalanche, earthquake, erosion, gravity, Himalayas, landslide, mudflows, penetrates, resort, rockfalls, rockslides, Rocky Mountains, saturated, seep, slab avalanche, slump, terrace, tsunami, vibration, volcano, wet snow avalanche

Blizzards

Young people usually look forward to the first snow of the season. The crisp air and beautiful **snow** enables them to take advantage of many activities such as skiing, sledding, making snow men, and throwing snowballs at one another. A gently falling snow, accompanied by moderate temperatures, makes a perfect day for enjoying one of natures wonders—a **snowstorm**. Occasionally, the snow does not fall gently and the temperatures are not moderate. It becomes very cold, and the winds are severe. When this happens, the snowstorm can turn into a **blizzard**. A blizzard is usually described as a heavy snowstorm with very cold temperatures and winds of at least 35 miles an hour.

You cannot go outside and play in a blizzard. It is too dangerous. Snow **accumulates** in drifts that block roads, bridges, and train tracks. Traffic is forced to stop. The snow collects on roofs, and sometimes must be scooped off so the roofs will not collapse under its weight. Blizzards interrupt electricity and communications. Emergency crews such as ambulances, fire fighters, policemen, and others may find it difficult to travel, and people often suffer.

Not only can blizzards cause a great deal of property damage, but they can also kill. Fortunately, blizzards are not common in the United States. When they do occur, it is usually in the northeastern regions. They have an even greater frequency in Russia and Canada. Although they are not common, blizzards are so dangerous, we must be careful if we are caught outside because of the hazards they present.

One major hazard is **hypothermia**. Hypothermia occurs when a person's body temperature drops below 95° because he or she is exposed to very cold air. The heart rate and the flow of blood is slowed. A person with hypothermia becomes very sleepy and is tempted to lie down and go to sleep. **Frostbite** is another hazard of blizzards. Skin that is exposed to cold air freezes, and this can cause permanent damage to parts of the body. Frostbite usually affects the fingers, toes, nose, or ears. The problem is made worse when the wind is blowing strongly and the **windchill** is lowered.

Another hazard is caused by the strong wind and blowing snow. People are sometimes unable to see during a blizzard and become lost and freeze to death. When snow is so heavy and driven by high winds that a person cannot see, it is called a **whiteout**. There are many stories of people who have become lost in a blizzard, were unable to find their way home, and have died. When the snow melts, they are sometimes discovered only a few feet from their own house. Many also die from **heart attacks** or **strokes**, as they shovel snow from their sidewalks or driveways.

People who have found protection in homes are sometimes also at risk. **Supplementary** heating systems, such as gas or kerosene heaters, can fail and give off poisonous fumes or cause fires. People in cars sometimes run their motors so that the heaters will keep them warm. If they are not careful, they can be at risk of **carbon monoxide** from the motor entering the passenger compartment. Carbon monoxide is a poisonous gas that is odorless.

Blizzards also may cause other weather problems. Snow builds up on the sides of mountains, and sometimes it may break loose and cascade to the lower levels. This is called an **avalanche**. Sometimes an avalanche occurs in the **wilderness** and does not pose a threat to humans. At other times, they occur in more populated areas, and when they come crashing down the mountain, they destroy homes and kill people.

Since blizzards bring immense quantities of snow, it must melt at some time and flow into rivers and streams. Slow melting snow usually does not cause a problem and is sometimes beneficial. The spring melt, which can cause a flood in some areas, provides the necessary **moisture** for growing grain in the northern plain states. States in the west depend on the melting snow to fill their **reservoirs** and provide water for drinking and farming. On the other hand, if the snow melts too rapidly and the spring rains are heavy, **flooding** can occur. This is one of the main causes of spring flooding.

Name _____ Date _____

Blizzard Vocabulary

How well do you understand the following terms dealing with blizzards? Below and to the left are a number of definitions. In the blank after each definition, write the word that is described by the definition. Use the terms given below.

Definition	**Term**
1. A heavy snowstorm accompanied by strong winds	_____
2. A condition in which blowing snow makes visibility impossible	_____
3. Very harsh	_____
4. An object revolving around the earth with weather instruments	_____
5. An instrument that finds things by bouncing radio waves	_____
6. A fence used along highways that traps falling and blowing snow	_____
7. A scientist who analyzes weather data	_____
8. To predict what will happen	_____
9. Rain, sleet, hail, or snow	_____
10. Dampness or wetness as vapor or condensation	_____
11. A very low body temperature	_____
12. Unsafe or dangerous	_____
13. A huge amount of snow that slides down the side of a mountain	_____
14. A federal agency that keeps weather records and makes forecasts	_____
15. A serious injury caused by exposure to extreme cold	_____
16. Death of body tissue, caused by insufficient blood supply	_____
17. To pile up or increase	_____
18. A highly poisonous gas that is colorless and odorless	_____
19. An overflowing of water onto dry land	_____
20. White, hexagonal ice crystals that fall in white flakes	_____
21. A term used to describe how cold air feels when blown by air	_____
22. Something added to make up for a deficiency	_____
23. A severe and sudden loss of brain function	_____
24. A serious medical problem due to a lack or reduced flow in the heart's blood supply	_____
25. Falling snow when it is not too cold and there is little wind	_____
26. An artificial lake used to store and regulate the flow of water	_____

accumulation, avalanche, blizzard, carbon monoxide, forecast, flooding, frostbite, gangrene, hazardous, heart attack, hypothermia, meteorologist, moisture, National Weather Service, precipitation, radar, reservoirs, satellite, severe, snow fence, snow, snowstorm, stroke, supplementary, whiteout, windchill

© Mark Twain Media, Inc., Publishers

White Out

BLIZZARD OF 1888

Sunday, March 11,1888, was a typical early spring day in New York, the largest city in the United States. Heavy rains soaked the area, and then about midnight, the rain turned into sleet and then into snow. Early in the morning on March 12, blizzard conditions started to form. Temperatures dropped quickly, the winds picked up, and the snow became more intense. While conditions were becoming dangerous, people still went about their business. People dressed warmly and trudged off to work. For most people in 1888, a day's pay was not something that could be lost simply because they did not want to get out in a snowstorm.

Before most could arrive at work, though, all forms of transportation were halted by the storm. Trains were blocked by snow drifts. The engineer on one train thought that a snow drift was no match for his "iron horse," so he gave the engine full throttle and tried to plow through the drift. The train derailed and four people were killed. Some passengers were stranded overnight and the following day without food or heat.

At this time, there were four elevated railroads in New York, which many people used to get to work. By noon, these trains were unable to move because of ice on the tracks, and the passengers were trapped high above the city with no heat and with no way to get down. It is estimated that 15,000 travelers were stranded on the elevated trains. Many were rescued, though, when several men on the ground found ladders and charged the passengers money to be rescued.

Those who chose to travel on the street did not fare any better. Horses had trouble pulling wagons and cabs. Streetcars, sometimes called trolleys, came off their tracks and the travelers were forced to leave the streetcars far from home in the middle of a blizzard. Many died trying to find shelter.

In addition to the suffering and death of the people, there was a great deal of property damage. Ice and wind broke telephone and telegraph wires. Gas and water pipes were also destroyed by the cold weather. Fortunately, the snow finally stopped falling on Tuesday, March 13. Over 20 inches of snow fell in New York, and Brooklyn had 26 inches, but the wind piled it up into deep drifts. In some cases, these drifts reached two stories high. Many drifts were just too deep to shovel away. Tunnels were cut through the biggest snowdrifts so people could walk down the sidewalks.

New York was not the only city to be affected by this record blizzard. However, most of the real problems occurred in New York because it was so heavily populated. The storm dropped record breaking snow totals all along the eastern seaboard. Saratoga Springs had 50 inches of snow. More than four feet of snow fell in the Albany and Troy areas of northeastern New York State. Similar amounts fell in areas like Middleton, Connecticut.

It took a week for life to return to normal. When it did, people began to assess the damage. It was estimated that over 400 people had frozen to death and that many of the deaths would not be revealed until the snow melted. About 200 ships along the eastern coast of the United States were sunk and 100 people were lost at sea. New York City alone lost over $20 million in property.

This blizzard caused officials to change their way of building in New York. After the blizzard, builders began burying pipes underground so that they would be protected from bad weather. The city also began plans for building an underground subway system, so that snow could not stop people from traveling.

> **DISASTER AT A GLANCE**
>
> **WHAT:** A devastating blizzard
>
> **WHERE:** Along the eastern seaboard
>
> **WHEN:** March 12, 1888
>
> **DEATHS:** 400.
>
> **COST:** Over $20 million in New York City
>
> **AFTERMATH:** Builders began burying water and gas pipes, and telephone and telegraph wires underground, so that they would be protected from bad weather. Plans began to build a subway that snow could not stop.

Name _____ Date _____

Check Your Knowledge of the Blizzard of 1888

Fill in the blanks in the following statements by using information from the narrative about the Blizzard of 1888.

1. There were four _____ in New York, which many used to get to work.

2. The person who drives a train is an _____.

3. A slang name for a train is an _____.

4. Another name for a trolley is _____.

5. The Blizzard of 1888 occurred on _____.

6. All forms of _____ were halted by the storm.

7. Trains were blocked by _____.

8. One train _____ and four people were killed.

9. Elevated trains were unable to move because of _____ on the tracks.

10. Many people on elevated trains were rescued by men with _____.

11. It is estimated that _____ travelers were stranded on the elevated trains.

12. _____ were cut through the biggest snowdrifts so people could walk down the sidewalks.

13. Ice and wind broke _____ and _____ wires.

14. _____ and _____ pipes were also destroyed by the cold weather.

15. It took a _____ for life to return to normal.

16. New York City alone lost over _____ in property.

17. The city also began plans for building an underground _____ system, so that snow could not stop people from traveling.

18. After the blizzard, builders began _____ water and gas pipes so that they would be protected from bad weather.

19. Over _____ people had frozen during the blizzard.

20. About _____ ships along the eastern coast of the United States were sunk.

21. About _____ people were lost at sea.

22. Most of the problems occurred in New York because it was heavily _____.

23. Saratoga Springs had _____ inches of snow.

24. The storm dropped record breaking snow totals all along the _____ seaboard.

25. Over _____ inches of snow fell in New York, and Brooklyn had _____ inches.

© Mark Twain Media, Inc., Publishers   28

Name _____ Date _____

Surviving a Blizzard

RESEARCH AND THINKING

In the spaces listed below, develop a plan to survive a blizzard.

1. What should I do to prepare in case of a blizzard? _____

_____

_____

_____

_____

2. If I am outdoors when a blizzard occurs, here is what I should do to survive. _____

_____

_____

_____

3. If I am indoors, here is what I should do to survive in a blizzard. _____

_____

_____

_____

4. If I am in a car, here is what I should do to survive in a blizzard. _____

_____

_____

_____

5. After a blizzard, here is what I should do. _____

_____

_____

_____

© Mark Twain Media, Inc., Publishers

A Dark and Deadly Shroud
The Valdez Oil Spill

On the night of March 23, 1989, the *Exxon Valdez,* one of the largest water vessels in the world, sat in the Alaskan port of Valdez. The thousand foot long oil tanker remained at the pipeline terminal until over 40 million gallons of oil had been pumped into its tank. At 9:26 p.m., after being fully loaded, the *Exxon Valdez* pulled away from the terminal and started on its five and a half day journey to Long Beach, California, where the oil was to be delivered.

Captain Joseph Hazelwood, who was considered one of the best commanders among those employed by Exxon, was in control of the *Valdez* that night. As the tanker approached Columbia Glacier, Captain Hazelwood noticed several icebergs floating in his path. In an effort to avoid the ice, he radioed the Coast Guard in Valdez and requested permission to change course. Since there were no other tankers in the area, the Coast Guard granted permission.

In order to "change lanes," Captain Hazelwood pointed the *Valdez* toward Bligh Reef. He then instructed Third Mate Gregory Cousins to turn the tanker back into the correct sea-lane once Busby Island was reached. After giving this final order, Hazelwood left the bridge and retired to his cabin.

Then, for some unknown reason, Cousins waited a full seven minutes before ordering the helmsman, who steers the vessel, to turn the vessel to the right. If Cousins had given the order sooner, the *Valdez* could have been maneuvered out of the channel successfully. Now, however, the ship was in serious trouble. Cousins, the helmsman and the rest of the crew quickly realized the *Valdez* would not be able to turn sharply enough to avoid the approaching reef.

Cousins immediately called Captain Hazelwood in his cabin and told him, "I think we're in serious trouble." As soon as he said these words, at approximately 12:04 a.m., Friday, March 24, 1989, the sound of grinding metal filled the night air, and the tanker experienced its first impact with Bligh Reef. The engines were immediately stopped, but the *Valdez,* needing a minimum of two miles to reach a complete stop, continued to move. As a result, the rocks of the reef tore through the hull of the ship, and the cargo of oil began spilling out into the sea.

It was 20 minutes before Hazelwood made the decision to radio the Coast Guard about what had occurred. When he finally did, he reported, "We've … it should be on your radar there … we've fetched up hard aground north of Goose Island off Bligh Reef. And, uh … evidently we're leaking some oil, and we're going to be here for a while."

He then began trying to free the tanker by trying to use the engines of the ship to thrust the *Valdez* across the reef.

> **DISASTER AT A GLANCE**
> **WHAT:** A tremendous oil spill
> **WHERE:** Prince William Sound
> **WHEN:** March 24, 1989
> **COST:** $20 million
> **AFTERMATH:** Thousands of animals died. The remnants of the spill exist today. While some measures to prevent future spills have been taken, they have been minor changes for the most part.

© Mark Twain Media, Inc., Publishers

However, this only managed to drive the rocks deeper into the ship, thus releasing more of the oil.

The oil then poured out so fast and furiously, it began to form a wave in the water that reached a height of three feet. The oil then began to spread out further into the sea.

At around 2:00 a.m., a crewman radioed the Coast Guard and reported that Captain Hazelwood had failed in his attempt to release the *Valdez* from the reef and the order was given to stop the engines once again.

During the first crucial days of the disaster, arguments raged over who should be responsible for the cleanup of the oil spill and what methods should be used. Meanwhile, the oil slick continued to grow larger each day.

By the third day, a massive storm hit Prince William Sound. As a result, the oil was blown onto the shore, creating a mousse (a brown mixture of oil and water). The oil still in the water now covered 500 square miles. And, because of the storm, most of the cleanup efforts that had been discussed would no longer work. In the end, the most common method of cleaning the shoreline was simply picking up individual rocks and wiping them off with absorbent towels. Still, it was impossible to completely clean up the spill, and residue from the great spill still remains today.

Although none of the crewmen had been injured in the impact, the wreck resulted in countless casualties. All wildlife in the area, including otters, seabirds, and fish, was immediately in danger. Most of the animals directly affected by the spill died. In fact, thousands of animals died in the first day alone.

Intent on saving the wildlife in the region, Exxon and several volunteer organizations set up bathing and medical clinics. Volunteers played a major part in the effort. Many even left their regular jobs in order to help rehabilitate the animals in need. While these volunteers were able to save the lives of many of the animal victims, a startling number still died. It is estimated that about one third of the birds (1,900) and half of the otters (200) could not be saved.

With so much at stake, it has become even more crucial to ensure that a spill like this does not happen again. Although, knowing the energy demands of the United States, it seems unlikely that oil will cease being pumped from the Valdez area. But, many believe steps can be taken to prevent a similar spill. Therefore, soon after the spill, the Alaska Oil Spill Commission (AOSC) was formed. Its job was to investigate the causes behind the Valdez oil spill and recommend preventative measures that could be taken against future spills.

In June 1989 the oil industry honored one of the many requests of the newly formed AOSC, and the Petroleum Industry Response Organization (PIRO) was created. PIRO then set up five regional centers for fighting oil spills. The centers are located at various points along the U.S. coastline and are intended to provide immediate response to oil spills occurring anywhere in the United States.

The AOSC also believes that future spills may be avoided by requiring tankers to be built with double hulls. But, as of yet, no laws have been passed by Congress.

Most laws that have been passed, though, concern higher standards for tanker personnel and the manner in which the tankers are operated. For instance, due to the controversy that surrounded Captain Hazelwood and speculations that he had been drunk, all captains must now take a breathalizer test within an hour before getting aboard the tanker. In addition, tankers are not allowed to change lanes anymore.

With all these precautions, chances of another catastrophic spill have been greatly reduced. However, no matter how many measures are taken, as long as oil is being transported, the reoccurrence of a spill such as the *Exxon Valdez* can never be eliminated.

Name _____ Date _____

Experiments With the Way Oil Spreads

What You Will Need:
- Spoon
- Eye dropper
- Pie pan
- Jar with lid
- Measuring cup
- Scale
- Vegetable oil
- Water

Fill the spoon to the rim with the vegetable oil, making sure not to let it spill over. Now, using your eye dropper, try adding more oil to the full spoon.

1. How does the oil behave in the spoon? _____

_____

2. Does it overflow immediately? _____

3. Are you able to add several drops of oil before the spoon overflows? _____

4. If so, how many? _____

5. Now, try to transfer the oil from the spoon to the jar, one drop at time. Can you do it?

_____

6. Pouring oil drop by drop is almost impossible because of surface tension. Each drop of oil is made up of millions of molecules, and surface tension is the tendency of these molecules to cling to each other. This is why you were able to keep adding oil to the spoon, even after it was full. This is also the way the oil behaved as it spilled into Prince William Sound.

7. Now, holding your pie pan at a 30-degree angle, try pouring $\frac{1}{3}$ cup of oil into the top end of the pan.

8. What happens to the oil in the pan? _____

_____

9. Does it stick together or spread out quickly? _____

_____

10. Now, pour equal amounts of oil and water into the jar.

11. How does the oil behave in relation to the water? _____

_____

_____

© Mark Twain Media, Inc., Publishers   32

Name _____ Date _____

12. Why do you think this is? _____

_____

13. Now, put the lid on the jar and shake it for several minutes.

14. What happened? _____

_____

15. How does the water and oil look? _____

_____

16. Did they combine or do they still seem to be separated? _____

_____

17. Why do you think this is? _____

_____

18. Let the jar sit undisturbed for 20 minutes.

19. How does the water and oil appear now? _____

_____

20. Why do you suppose this is? _____

_____

21. Using the scale, weigh a cup of water, then a cup of oil. Do they weigh the same? _____

22. If not, which liquid is heavier? _____

23. Does this explain how the oil and water behaved in the jar? _____

24. How? _____

_____

25. Using your findings, discuss why the properties of oil may make it easier or more difficult to clean up after a spill.

_____

_____

Name _____ Date _____

Experiments in Cleaning Up Oil Spills

What You Will Need:

- A large pan (at least 2 inches deep)
- Measuring cup
- Motor oil
- A paint stirrer
- Sand
- A rock
- A shell
- A stick or a block of wood

- Material that resembles fur
- A feather
- Straw
- Paper towel
- Tap water
- Hot water
- Dish washing detergent
- Cotton cloth

Follow these steps.

1. In the pan, build a beach by sloping the sand up one end.
2. Take the rock, shell, wood, fur, and feather and push them all securely into the sand.
3. Slowly pour the tap water into the pan until it reaches about halfway up the "beach."
4. Measure $\frac{1}{2}$ cup of the motor oil and pour it into the opposite end of the pan.
5. Using the paint stirrer, create waves in the water, washing the oil over all of the objects you have placed there.
6. Repeat.

Answer the following questions.

1. How did the oil stick to the different objects on the beach? _____

_____

2. Did some seem to be more coated with oil than others? _____

_____

3. Did the oil stick to the sand? _____

4. If so, did it stay on the surface, or did the sand absorb it? _____

_____

5. Using your objects coated with oil as guide, how do you think this oil will affect the environment and wildlife?

_____

_____

_____

Name _____ Date _____

6. Now it is time to try to clean up the mess. Using the straw, paper towel, hot water, dish washing detergent, and cotton cloth, try to clean the items that have oil on them. Try different methods of cleaning on each item.

7. How effective were the different methods of cleaning the "shoreline" and the "wildlife"?

_____

_____

8. Which ones worked best? _____

_____

9. Did different methods have better results when used on different items? _____

_____

_____

10. Which items were the hardest to clean? _____

_____

11. Why do you think that is? _____

_____

12. How long do you think it would take to clean up a shoreline such as Prince William Sound (more than 1,000 miles of individual rocks and shells and thousands of otters and seabirds) using the methods you tried?

_____

13. Do you think it could ever be completely cleaned using these methods? _____

_____

14. Why or why not? _____

_____

_____

Methods similar to the ones you tried were used to try to clean the beach around Prince William Sound. And, although teams worked for six months and these methods were considered effective, it is estimated that only about 20 percent of the oil was removed from the shoreline in this way.

Name _____ Date _____

What Went Wrong?

When conservationists found out the Trans-Atlantic pipeline was to be built through Prince William Sound, an area known for its abundance of wildlife and plant life, they were very upset. They battled to have the pipeline built across Canada and into the Midwest. Although they lost the battle, the state of Alaska guaranteed them that everything would be done to prevent a major oil spill in the area.

The state required Alyeska, the company that runs the pipeline, to provide a detailed plan of what would be done if a major spill were to occur. Alyeska then came up with a plan that described all the equipment that would be used and where this equipment was located. It even went so far as to list the phone numbers of the people that would be called in the event of a spill.

However, when the *Exxon Valdez* oil spill finally did occur, no one seemed prepared. As a result, irreparable damage was done to Prince William Sound and the surrounding area—much of which could have been prevented. Using sources at your local library and on the Internet, research what went wrong. Explain what you think the major mistakes were in the cleanup effort and how things could have been handled differently. What would you have done if you had been in charge? Could you have saved the area?

_____

_____

_____

_____

_____

_____

_____

_____

_____

_____

_____

_____

_____

_____

When the Lights Dimmed in the Ukraine
THE CHERNOBYL DISASTER

On April 26, 1986, at 1:23 a.m., operators at the Chernobyl nuclear power plant in the Ukrainian Socialist Republic noticed that the core of the nuclear reactor had begun to severely overheat. Then, less than one minute later, two explosions took place. One was a steam explosion, and the other was caused by the expansion of fuel vapor. As a result, the graphite moderator blocks mixed with the outside air, forming highly flammable carbon monoxide, resulting in a deadly fire. Subsequently, a mass of radioactive dust was released into the atmosphere and carried across Soviet borders and into much of Europe.

Several seconds later, 30 fires were ripping through the plant. Minutes later, the plant's fire fighters arrived and tried desperately to control the fire, but their attempts proved futile. By 3:30 a.m., firefighters from surrounding towns had joined the heroic effort. By April 28, officials had begun the evacuation of the surrounding towns. Over 1,100 buses and military trucks were sent from Kiev to transport the 49,000 residents, along with their 19,000 cattle and pets. Then, on May 2, the village of Chernobyl was evacuated. By the time the evacuation was completed, 135,000 people, residing in 179 towns, had been told to leave their homes.

Finally, two weeks later, the firefighters succeeded in smothering the fire. But the disaster was far from over. In all, approximately eight of the 140 tons of fuel, containing plutonium and other extremely radioactive materials, were released from the reactor. A section of the graphite moderator, which is radioactive, was also expelled and scattered throughout the surrounding area.

At least 30 people died immediately as a result of receiving large doses of radiation on the day of the explosion, but it is impossible to predict how many more will die. Radiation from the explosion continues to cause cancer in people who were exposed to it. Experts estimate that by the year 2036, at least another 7,000 people will be affected by it.

Also, much of the radiation was absorbed into the soil and, ultimately, by the surrounding plants. These plants are then eaten by animals, which in turn are eaten by humans, once again causing exposure to the lethal radiation. Experts believe this radioactive material may remain in the soil for several decades. As a result, it is estimated that up to 40,000 people could die or become ill within the next 70 years.

In addition, farmers have suffered a huge economic loss. Sweden and Norway, however, are playing a huge role in the economic relief effort. They spend over $20 million a year buying contaminated meat. After the meat is purchased, it is immediately destroyed, making sure no one will suffer from its consumption.

In a massive effort to contain the radioactive material, Soviet engineers designed a sarcophagus, a huge concrete box that entombs the remains of the reactor. However, many experts now fear that it is on the brink of collapse. As a result, several plans for providing a sturdy, permanent structure are being reviewed.

Shortly after the accident, a Soviet antinuclear movement was formed. Their main objective is to ensure that nuclear accidents, such as the one at Chernobyl, are forever avoided.

DISASTER AT A GLANCE

WHAT: An overheated nuclear power plant explodes, releasing radioactive dust into the Soviet Union and Europe.

WHERE: The Chernobyl nuclear power plant in the Ukrainian Socialist Republic

WHEN: April 26, 1986

DEATHS: Unknown. At least 30 died immediately. Experts estimate that by the year 2036, at least another 7,000 people will be affected.

AFTERMATH: A Soviet antinuclear movement was formed to ensure that nuclear accidents are avoided.

Name _____ Date _____

Chernobyl Vocabulary

How well do you understand the following terms dealing with nuclear accidents? Below and to the left are a number of definitions. In the blank after each definition, write the word that is described by the definition. Use the terms given below.

Definition	**Term**
1. An instrument that detects and measures the amount of radiation present	_____
2. A type of energy derived from reactions in an atom's nuclei	_____
3. In this process, atomic nuclei release particles that split the nuclei of other atoms and may lead to a chain reaction.	_____
4. A type of cancer that is found in the bone marrow	_____
5. Energy that is derived from nuclear reactions	_____
6. The large, concrete structure used to entomb the remains of the nuclear reactor at Chernobyl.	_____
7. This happens when a nuclear reactor's fuel burns through its containers and is absorbed into the ground.	_____
8. A highly radioactive element that is produced as a result of nuclear fission reactions	_____
9. Unstable atoms give off these particles	_____
10. In this process, two atoms are forced together and form a new heavier atom and release energy	_____
11. Nuclear reactions take place in this device	_____
12. This is the most commonly used material for nuclear fuel	_____
13. The nickname commonly given to a nuclear meltdown	_____
14. Exposure to large amounts of radiation can result in this illness	_____
15. Central part of a nuclear reactor, where fission reactions occur	_____
16. The center of an atom, where protons and neutrons are	_____

atomic energy, cesium-137, China syndrome, core, Geiger counter, leukemia, meltdown, nuclear energy, nuclear fusion, nuclear fission, nuclear reactor, nucleus, radiation, radiation sickness, sarcophagus, uranium-235

Name _____ Date _____

Extinguish a Fire

What You Will Need:

- A tea candle
- Matches or lighter
- 2 empty glasses
- Teaspoon full of baking soda
- Vinegar

Follow these steps.

1. Put the tea candle in one of the empty glasses.
2. Using the matches or the lighter, light the candle.
3. In the other glass, mix the baking soda with the vinegar, allowing it to foam.
4. Slowly tilt the glass with the mixture over the candle.

Answer the following questions.

1. What happened? _____

_____

_____

2. Why do you think this happened? _____

_____

_____

_____

_____

_____

© Mark Twain Media, Inc., Publishers

A Blight Upon the Land

THE IRISH POTATO FAMINE

Each year on March 17 we celebrate one of the most festive and happy holidays of the year. St. Patrick's Day is an Irish holiday honoring the missionary credited with converting the Irish to Christianity. In the United States, St. Patrick's Day is a time when almost everyone says they are at least part Irish. People wear green, sing, dance, eat, drink, and basically have a good time. If a person looked at this celebration, they would conclude that the Irish were a carefree people without problems who sang and danced all day long. They would be wrong. In fact, the Irish people have suffered terribly throughout their history.

Ireland is a small island just to the west of England. The two countries are separated by the Irish Sea. Ireland has been invaded by various groups throughout the ages, but it wasn't until 1171 when King Henry II of England took control of the country, that British rule began and has continued for over 700 years. As is common when one country invades another, Britain began taxing the Irish heavily. This is the same thing that occurred in America, and eventually led to the American Revolution and our break with Britain.

The Irish, however, were unable to successfully defy the British militarily. They were very close to the invading country, so reinforcements could be sent rather quickly. They were also a very poor country. All they basically had was their land and their crops. And the best of the crops—mainly grains such as wheat and barely—were sent to Britain as a form of taxation. As a result, most Irish lived a life of constant work and hunger. But, as difficult as the life of the Irish was, it would get worse.

In the 1500s King Henry VIII split Britain from the Roman Catholic church and established the King of England as the head of the Church of England. He decreed that all of the lands under British rule also denounce the Catholic church and adopt the new protestant church he had established. This was difficult for the Irish people. They had little in their life but their Catholic religion. Catholicism had been part of their culture since 432, when a priest named Patrick came to Ireland and converted most of the people from paganism to Catholicism.

Those that defied the king and continued to follow their Catholic religion were severely punished. There were special laws passed not only against practicing the Catholic religion, but against being a Catholic. Those that defied the laws were dealt with harshly. Perhaps the most outrageous punishment was taking the farms away from the Irish. The wealthy Britons who took the land let the previous Irish owners live on and work the farms, but they could not own the land or anything it produced. Irish farmers were required to give the crops and livestock to the new British owners as rent. In some cases, the farmers sold the crops and sent the proceeds to the landowners. Irish farmers would not have been able to survive had it not been for the one crop they were able to grow—potatoes.

Potatoes were the salvation of the Irish. Not a native plant of Ireland, the Spanish brought potatoes to Europe from South America, and they eventually made their way to Ireland. It was an ideal crop for this poor country. While the large fields were used to plant crops for the British landlords, every other available spot was used to plant potatoes. In yards,

DISASTER AT A GLANCE
WHAT: A famine caused by a fungus destroyed the potato crop, a staple of the Irish diet.
WHERE: Ireland
WHEN: 1845–1849
DEATHS: More than a million died of starvation and fever.
AFTERMATH: Ireland's population dropped from 8 million to 5 million. About 800,000 were evicted from their homes. Nearly 2 million emigrated. There was an increase in the hatred for England.

© Mark Twain Media, Inc., Publishers

around the house, in the woods—wherever there was a little land, someone would plant potatoes. The potato is a high-yield plant, so only a single acre of land could produce enough food for a family of four. When combined with butter and milk, potatoes were enough to sustain the Irish for many generations. These "spuds" or "lumpers," as they were called, had one shortcoming. They could not be stored for long because potatoes spoiled quickly. The farmers needed to have a good crop every year in order to survive.

Occasionally, there were crop failures, and thousands of people died of starvation. Fortunately, the next year the crop was usually good again, and the people survived. However, this changed in 1845. The potato crop the Irish depended on was hit with a fungus called *Phytophthora infestans* that rotted almost 40 percent of the potato crop. The fungus was called the "**blight**," and it turned the potato stalks black within a matter of days and made the fields a sea of rotting vegetables giving off a putrid odor. As devastating as this crop failure was, the next year was even worse. In 1846 the entire crop of potatoes was destroyed by the fungus. The potato crops from 1847 to 1851 were unaffected by the blight, but the famine conditions brought about by the blight still caused problems. In 1847 there were not many seed potatoes to plant new crops, and many farmers did not plant because they thought the crop would be destroyed by the blight anyway.

These were the darkest days for the Irish. The price of food soared. People went into the woods to find food. Some existed by eating birds, grass, or any plant they could find. Others tried to eat the potatoes with the blight, but became sick and died. Hunger and disease killed entire families. Eventually, more than one million people died. There were so many bodies and so little money for coffins, that many weren't even buried. They were just thrown in open ditches. The survivors were too weak from hunger to cover the bodies.

Many of the crops the farmers used to pay the rent to their landlords were also destroyed, but others were not. The farmers that grew these successful crops that were to be sent to the British landlords had a tough choice to make. Do they send the crops and let their own families starve, or do they eat the crops and have the landlords evict them from the land because they did not send the crops as a payment for their rent? Landlords eventually evicted hundreds of thousands of peasants and tore the Irish families' cottages down. This was called **tumbling**.

At this time, the British believed in a ***laissez-faire*** economic philosophy. This is a philosophy that believes that the government should not interfere and let natural economic forces control the economy. Therefore, the government initially did little to help the starving Irish. They also felt the Irish were inferior and not worthy of the effort to help them. Eventually, however, there were a few low-paid working projects established to provide much needed jobs, as well as other forms of assistance, but the Irish felt the British provided too little too late.

The Irish Potato Famine affected not only Ireland and Britain, but also the entire world. Many Irish men and women looking for a better life emigrated to other countries. Nearly two million Irish came to the United States during the 1840s and 1850s. Even their decision to emigrate caused additional hardships. The unstable ships they sailed on were called "**coffin ships**", and as many as one-third to one-half of the passengers died of hunger and disease during the passage. It is reported that sharks followed these ships waiting for the dead bodies to be tossed overboard.

When the Irish arrived in America, they did not find the promised land they had hoped for. They expected a life free from prejudice and hatred in a new country. While the country was new, the people in the new country showed the same prejudice and hatred the British exhibited. Americans, feeling that the Irish were going to take their jobs, did not welcome them with open arms. Many factories put signs on the front doors that read, "Irish Need Not Apply."

The famine, disease, and the emigration that followed lowered the population of Ireland from eight million before the famine to five million. It also caused a rise in Irish nationalism and an anger against the British that still exists today.

Name_____ Date _____

Check Your Knowledge of Ireland and the Famine

1. A _____ was an unstable vessel that carried Irish emigrants to other countries.

2. A _____ is a crop that produces a high yield from a small space.

3. The economic theory that believed that the government should not become involved in business is called _____ .

4. The two slang names the Irish used for potatoes were _____ and _____.

5. _____ is the scientific name for the fungus that caused the Potato Famine.

6. The common name for the potato fungus is _____.

7. _____ is the process of evicting a family and tearing down their cottage.

8. The priest who converted most of the Irish from paganism to Catholicism was named _____.

9. A heathen is a person without religion. He is sometimes called a _____.

10. A _____ is an Irish fairy that looks like a small, old man.

11. Kissing the _____ is supposed to make the kisser eloquent.

12. A holiday celebrated on March 17 is called _____.

13. Sometimes called the national emblem of Ireland, the _____ has three leaf-lets like a clover.

14. _____ is the color most often associated with Ireland.

15. Ireland is a small island just to the _____ of England.

16. _____ split Britain from the Roman Catholic church and established the King of England as the head of the Church of England.

17. _____ were the staple food for the Irish.

18. The _____ brought potatoes to Europe.

19. The potato is native to _____.

20. England and Ireland are separated by the _____.

21. People who rent land or buildings to others are called _____.

22. A single acre of land planted in potatoes could produce enough food for a family of _____.

23. Another name for a small farmer, sharecropper, or laborer where they are the primary labor force in agriculture is _____.

24. A _____ is a severe food shortage.

© Mark Twain Media, Inc., Publishers

Black Blizzard

DUST BOWL DROUGHT OF THE 1930S

For countless centuries, the center of the North American continent has been an **immense semiarid** grassland we now know as the Great Plains. **Fossils** and **marine deposits** reveal that in **prehistoric** times, the Great Plains was actually part of a huge inland sea that vanished long ago. The water was eventually replaced by a sea of grass. The wind, **unfettered** by huge mountains, sweeps across the **plains** causing the grass to ripple and wave, much like the water does on a lake. The land, for the most part, is level, except for small, **localized** hills. The **precipitation** on the plains averages about 20 inches per year, but this average drops considerably in the western and southern parts. With the strong winds and the great **variations** in temperature, one would think that little life would exist in this **region**. However, this is not true.

A variety of insects, mice, prairie dogs, jackrabbits, rattlesnakes, weasels, badgers, coyotes, wolves, pronghorn antelope, grizzlies, prairie chickens, hawks, eagles, and even the buffalo found the plains a **hospitable** place to eat and live. Each of these creatures, in some way, lived off the great sea of grass that **blanketed** the area. Insects and small **herbivores**, such as mice, jackrabbits, and prairie dogs, ate the grass. In turn, the insects and the small animals provided food for the larger **predators**, known as **carnivores**. Even the **magnificent** buffalo lived off the grass. They would eat part way down the stalk and then move on. **Nomadic Native Americans** would follow the huge herd of buffalo, killing them for food, hides, and bones. It might be said that every **species**, in one way or another, depended on the grasses of the prairie for life. Loss of the grasses would be disastrous for the plains, because they provided more than just food and shelter for the creatures, they literally held the plains together. In order to understand its true importance to the plains, one must understand how wild grasses live and grow.

Wild grasses are **perennial** plants that continue growing each year. Over a period of time, the wild grasses in the southern plains developed a system of roots that **burrowed** deep into the earth, so that the grass could **survive** long periods of **drought**. These roots formed a thick, heavy covering on the topsoil called **sod** that covered the plains much like a blanket. The sod prevented the wind from blowing the **topsoil** away, and it also prevented the water from **eroding** it. It had an additional benefit, too. Since rainfall is so **sparse** in some areas, the sod was able to capture what little moisture there was and keep it from **evaporating**.

As a result, the prairie **ecosystem** was in perfect balance or **equilibrium**. It was like a long chain, with each creature representing a link. **Ecologists** point out if one takes away one link, the chain is broken. **Eliminate** one group of creatures, and the food cycle is broken. For example, if there were no predators to eat and manage the small rodents of the grasslands, they could multiply unrestricted, and eventually their **voracious** appetites for grass and grain could destroy all of the grassland. An ecosystem is delicate, but nature has a way of keeping it balanced so that all **organisms** can survive.

The first group to upset the equilibrium was the white hunters. In the latter part of the nineteenth century, demand

---

DISASTER AT A GLANCE

WHAT: One of the most significant droughts in American history

WHERE: Centered on the Oklahoma panhandle, it included parts of Nebraska, Kansas, Texas, New Mexico, and Colorado.

WHEN: The 1930s

WHY: Drought and destruction of the natural ecological system

AFTERMATH: Many farmers of the dust bowl moved to California. The federal government taught the farmers who remained new farming methods and techniques to preserve the land.

for fur made buffalo hunting a **lucrative** occupation. The huge animals were easy targets as a hunter **reclined** on a hill and shot them. A hunter could kill over 200 buffalo a day. For the most part, the hunter took only the hides, and the rest of the buffalo was left to **decompose** or for **scavengers** to eat. In just a few years, the great buffalo herds of the plains were gone, and the Native Americans who fought the white intruders in order to keep their way of life were placed on **reservations**.

The next group of white settlers to come to the Great Plains were ranchers. The large **expanse** of grasslands made ideal **grazing** land for their cattle. At first, the cattle ranchers **prospered** in this area. But in an effort to make more money, they continued the **assault** on the ecosystem. They killed the remaining buffalo and pronghorn antelope that were competing with their cattle for grass. They killed grizzlies, wolves, eagles, and other predators that would attack their livestock. As a consequence, grasshoppers, mice, jackrabbits, and prairie dogs **thrived** and multiplied, since there were fewer animals to prey on them. These creatures ate **relentlessly**, and along with the cattle, they all but eliminated the grass. The shortage of grass and a severe winter in 1886–1887 caused most ranchers to **abandon** the plains.

The rancher's **departure** was a signal for the farmers to come to the plains. In order to plant their crops, farmers needed to break through the strong sod that covered the fields. This sod was so strong that farmers were able to cut it into squares and make homes out of it. While **stripping** the sod from the land enabled the farmers to plant their crops, it also made the earth **vulnerable** to **erosion**. The farmers thought since the grass grew in such **abundance**, wheat and corn would also grow well in this area. They were right. But wheat and corn are different from the **native** grasses in one important way. They are **annuals**, not perennials. Since they needed to be planted each year, they did not have such a deep and **elaborate** rooting system. With no sod to keep the soil from eroding once the crop was **harvested**, the soil could be lost because of the wind and rain.

For many years, the farmers in this region **flourished**. World War I increased the demand for wheat, and the farmers met that demand by plowing more fields. **Mechanization** of farms made farmers so **productive**, that after the war, the price of wheat dropped. A lower price encouraged the farmers to plow even more fields to grow more in order to make up for the lower price.

Then drought began in 1931. There was little rain. Dust storms, called **black blizzards**, became frequent. Topsoil, along with the seed planted in it, was blown away. Dust clouds a thousand feet high **obscured** the sun. Dust covered the roads like huge snowdrifts. It covered rail lines and **disrupted** air travel all the way to Chicago. Houses were shut up and made as tight as possible. The cracks under the doors were sealed, but still the dust made its way in. People tied handkerchiefs over their noses and wore goggles. Eventually, an area that included the panhandles of Texas and Oklahoma, and parts of Nebraska, Kansas, Colorado, and New Mexico was named the **Dust Bowl**, because it was the most severely affected.

Constantly breathing dust caused many health problems—**bronchitis**, strep throat, and an illness called **dust pneumonia**. The problem persisted for about 10 years. Many lost their farms when banks **foreclosed** on their **mortgages**. Some farmers moved to California to find a better life. But the **Okies**, as they were called, were not welcomed, and the only work they could get was as laborers on huge **corporate farms**.

The federal government began many programs to help the farmers that remained on the plains. Many of the programs were unsuccessful, but some helped. Government **agronomists** encouraged farmers to adopt soil-saving farming techniques, such as **contour plowing**, **crop diversity**, **terracing**, **windbreaks,** and **crop rotation**. So far, these techniques have proved effective in slowing **runoff** of rainwater and improving its **absorption** into the soil. But the valuable topsoil that has already been lost to erosion is gone forever.

© Mark Twain Media, Inc., Publishers

Name_____ Date _____

Research and Thinking for the Dust Bowl

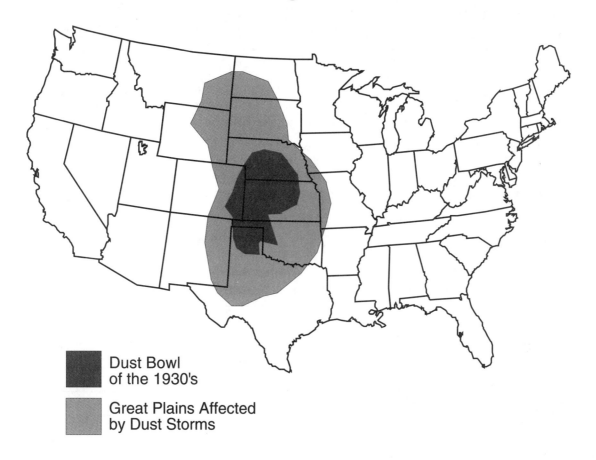

Dust Bowl of the 1930's

Great Plains Affected by Dust Storms

1. What states were included in the Dust Bowl of the 1930s?_____

_____

2. What states were affected by the dust storms during this era?_____

_____

_____

3. Using your library or by doing research on the Internet, read firsthand accounts of people who experienced the dust storms in the 1930s. Imagine you are a young person living on a farm in the dust bowl during the 1930s. On a separate sheet of paper, write a letter to your uncle who lives in New York. The first part of your letter should specifically describe what is happening to your family farm, and the second part of your letter should explain why it is occurring.

4. Imagine you are the same person as described in #3. Write an entry in your diary that describes your encounter with a dust storm as you were walking home from town.

Name _____ Date _____

Dust Bowl Vocabulary

How well do you understand the following terms dealing with the Dust Bowl? Below and to the left are a number of definitions. In the blank after each definition, write the word that is described by the definition. Use the terms given at the end of the exercise.

Definition	**Term**
1. An expert in crop production and soil management	_____
2. Plowing to stop erosion by following the natural lines of slopes and ridges	_____
3. The group of all organisms in a specific environment	_____
4. The top layer of soil containing the roots and grasses	_____
5. Plowing to stop erosion; plowing is done in levels on a hill	_____
6. A state of balance	_____
7. A classification for a group of similar organisms capable of inter-breeding	_____
8. A relatively narrow strip of land that is part of a state	_____
9. An area that has less than 10 inches of rain annually	_____
10. A respiratory infection caused by dust storms	_____
11. Planting a barrier of trees or shrubs to protect crops from strong winds	_____
12. An animal that feeds on plants	_____
13. Derogatory term for migrants leaving the Dust Bowl	_____
14. A long period of dry weather	_____
15. Deals with breathing	_____
16. Has no permanent home; wanders from place to place	_____
17. A plant that lasts for many years	_____
18. The conditions that affect the nature of an individual or a community	_____
19. A period of a poor economy and unemployment	_____
20. A farm laborer who moves from one farm to another	_____
21. A plant that lives for only one growing season	_____
22. Wearing away the soil by wind or water	_____
23. An animal that eats meat	_____
24. The practice of producing a variety of products, not just a single crop	_____
25. A large farm owned by many people	_____
26. A layer of fossils that originally lived in water	_____

© Mark Twain Media, Inc., Publishers

Name _____ Date _____

27. The group of people who lived here before white settlers; some- _____
times referred to as Indians

28. A scientist who studies the relationship between an organism and _____
its environment

29. A form of life _____

30. A creature that feeds off decaying matter _____

31. An area set aside for use by Native Americans _____

32. To rot _____

33. To feed on grass _____

34. The science of the relationship between an organism and its _____
environment

35. The process of gathering a crop _____

36. To produce with machines _____

37. A slang term given to harsh dust storms _____

38. A 150,000 square-mile area that included parts of Texas, Okla- _____
homa, Nebraska, Kansas, Colorado, and New Mexico

39. Relating to the tubes leading to the lungs _____

40. The process of changing the type of crop on a specific part of land _____
each year

agronomist, annual, black blizzard, bronchial, carnivore, contour plowing, corporate farm, crop rotation, decompose, diversify, drought, Dust Bowl, dust pneumonia, ecologist, ecology, ecosystem, environment, equilibrium, erode, graze, Great Depression, harvest, herbivore, marine deposits, mechanization, migrant worker, Native Americans, nomadic, Okie, organism, panhandle, perennial, reservation, respiratory, scavenger, semiarid, shelter belt, sod, species, terracing

© Mark Twain Media, Inc., Publishers

Name _____ Date _____

Improving Your Vocabulary

Read each of the following sentences that have been adapted from the information on the Dust Bowl. Below each sentence are four words. One of these words is a synonym for the word that is in bold print. Circle the word that most nearly matches, and write a sentence of your own that uses the word in bold type.

1. The center of the North American continent was an **immense** semiarid grassland.
   A. dry   B. large   C. submerged   D. small

2. The wind, **unfettered** by huge mountains, sweeps across the plains.
   A. unrestricted   B. crowded   C. small   D. nearby

3. The land is level, except for small, **localized** hills.
   A. short   B. unrestricted   C. little   D. isolated

4. Creatures found the plains a **hospitable** place to eat and live.
   A. cordial   B. dry   C. hostile   D. arid

5. The plains have strong winds and great **variations** in temperature.
   A. humid   B. variety   C. limited   D. high

6. Each creature lived off the great sea of grass that **blanketed** the area.
   A. decorated   B. fed   C. warmed   D. covered

7. Mechanization made farmers **productive.**
   A. pleasant   B. happy   C. ineffective   D. efficient

8. The wild grasses developed a system of roots that **burrowed** deep into the earth
   A. emerged   B. grew   C. collapsed   D. crumpled

9. Deep roots enable grasses to **survive** long periods of drought.
   A. last   B. bond   C. increase   D. rise

10. The rainfall is **sparse** in some areas.
    A. meager   B. plentiful   C. heavy   D. wet

11. The sod is able to capture what little moisture there is and keep it from **evaporating**.
    A. accumulating   B. spilling   C. vaporizing   D. collecting

12. **Eliminate** one group of creatures and the food cycle is broken.
    A. remove   B. count   C. annex   D. breed

© Mark Twain Media, Inc., Publishers   48

Name _____ Date _____

13. Their **voracious** appetite for grass and grain could destroy all of the grassland.
    A. trifling   B. minuscule   C. changeable   D. greedy

14. The demand for fur made buffalo hunting a **lucrative** occupation.
    A. lucid   B. profitable   C. unprofitable   D. meager

15. The huge animals were easy targets as a hunter **reclined** on a hill and shot them.
    A. walked   B. lay   C. stood   D. paced

16. The plains were a large **expanse** of grasslands.
    A. caged   B. fenced   C. space   D. cooped

17. At first, the cattle ranchers **prospered** in this area.
    A. despaired   B. cracked   C. collapsed   D. flourished

18. They continued the **assault** on the ecosystem.
    A. retreat   B. attack   C. harbor   D. refuse

19. As a consequence, the creatures **thrived** and multiplied.
    A. flourished   B. divided   C. died   D. faded

20. These creatures ate **relentlessly**.
    A. slowly   B. haltingly   C. continuously   D. intermittently

21. The severe winter caused most ranchers to **abandon** the plains.
    A. seed   B. plow   C. leave   D. visit

22. The ranchers' **departure** was a signal for the farmers to come to the plains.
    A. invitation   B. destination   C. arrival   D. leaving

23. Dust clouds a thousand feet high **obscured** the sun.
    A. brightened   B. dimmed   C. focused   D. reflected

24. Stripping the sod made the earth **vulnerable** to erosion.
    A. invincible   B. unconquerable   C. susceptible   D. impossible

25. The grass grew in **abundance**.
    A. plenty   B. sparse   C. meager   D. height

26. Dust covered rail lines and **disrupted** air travel all the way to Chicago.
    A. increased   B. boosted   C. encouraged   D. hampered

© Mark Twain Media, Inc., Publishers

Earthquakes

A sudden movement or vibration of the earth's **crust** or surface is called an **earthquake**. While earthquakes can be very destructive and cause a great deal of damage and loss of life, many are so minor that they go unnoticed. In fact, it is estimated that there are over 1,000 earthquakes every day, caused by the release of pressure along geologic **faults** or by volcanic activity inside the earth.

To understand why earthquakes occur, one must understand the **continental drift** theory. As you have learned in geography class, there are seven continents: Africa, Antarctica, Asia, Australia, Europe, North America, and South America. If you look at a map of the globe and note the shape of the continents, you will see that the shape of one continent looks as if it could have been cut out of the one just opposite it. The continents look like, if you could shove them together, they could almost form one large mass. This is exactly what a German **meteorologist**, Alfred Wegener, observed in 1912. His theory was that, at some time in the past, all of the land was connected and formed one large landmass. While many scientists ridiculed his original announcement, other scientists, such as **paleontologists**, were less skeptical. They said that Wegener's theory would explain why similar **fossils** of **prehistoric** creatures are found on every continent. They felt that many of these creatures could not have crossed the ocean from one continent to the other, and it was unlikely that identical creatures could have evolved independently on different continents.

The next obvious question that one asks is, "If the continents were once all connected, what has separated them?" In order to understand the answer to this question, one must understand the earth and its several parts. The earth is not just one solid piece of rock and soil, as it appears. The earth consists of several layers of different materials. The center of the earth is called the **core**. The **inner core** of the earth is composed of solid metal, while the **outer core** is hot and partly molten. The layer surrounding the outer core consists of hot rocks that are partially melted and is called the **mantle**. The outer layer of the earth is called the crust. The crust is the cool soil and rock that humans can see and live on.

While the crust appears to be one continuous piece of material, it is not. The crust is composed of several sheets, or **tectonic plates**, that are not connected. Not only are they not connected, they are not fixed. The hot rock and the mantle below the crust moves these plates up and down and also toward or away from each other. Therefore, continents on these plates may shift or drift one to four inches per year. When the plates drift away from each other, the continents separate as they are today. But when the plates drift toward each other, they sometimes collide with one another. The pressure caused by this constant shifting of the plates causes earthquakes.

Earthquakes occur along **faults**. A fault is the separation between two plates. They are the edges where two plates meet. When the pressure builds between two plates so much that the earth's crust is broken, there is an earthquake. A famous fault in the United States is the **San Andreas fault**, which runs through California. This fault was the location of one of the most devastating earthquakes in the United States—the 1906 San Francisco Earthquake. Another well-known earthquake along this fault occurred in 1989.

Earthquakes occur frequently in the countries that rim the Pacific Ocean. This area is called the **Ring of Fire** since it contains active volcanoes. Earthquakes in this area are usually caused by the movement of the hot melted rock, called **magma**, which is located inside the earth.

When an earthquake occurs, the ground trembles and **undulates** and cracks appear in the earth. Buildings, bridges, and other structures may collapse or become damaged. Scientists can sometimes predict an earthquake before it occurs, because there are small **tremors** before the major quake. These small tremors are called **foreshocks**. While an earthquake may not last very

© Mark Twain Media, Inc., Publishers

50

long, there are usually several **aftershocks** that may occur days, weeks, or even months after the main quake. However, the initial **shock wave** and the aftershocks do not cause all of the destruction associated with an earthquake. There are usually fires, sometimes called **conflagrations**, caused by broken gas lines, accidents caused by unstable buildings and structures, and hysteria among the survivors.

Other consequences of an earthquake are not as apparent. A very destructive earthquake can give dishonest people the opportunity to **loot** stores and private homes. In addition, following an underwater earthquake or a quake near the ocean, there may be an enormous wave, called a **tsunami**, that can destroy cities along the shore. Earthquakes can also cause **landslides** and **avalanches**.

In order to discover the force of a particular earthquake, **seismologists** use an instrument called a **seismograph**. The seismograph measures not only the strength and length of the earthquake, it also measures the amount of movement and locates the **focus** and **epicenter** of the quake. The information gathered by the seismograph is used to determine the power of the earthquake. The scale used to discover the power or **magnitude** of earthquakes was developed by Charles Richter, an American seismologist. An earthquake that measures less than 5 on the **Richter Scale** is not considered a major earthquake, since it would cause little damage. An earthquake that measures over 7 on the Richter Scale, however, would be considered a major earthquake.

Famous Earthquakes in History

Date	Information
1556 China	The most deadly earthquake in history—830,000 killed
1811 New Madrid, Missouri	The largest series of earthquakes in North America
1906 San Francisco	The most famous American earthquake, it left San Francisco in ruins.
1908 Messina, Sicily	The city was totally destroyed—85,000 killed.
1920 China	200,000 killed
1923 Japan	140,000 killed
1939 Turkey	100,000 killed
1964 Alaska	The strongest earthquake to strike North America
1976 China	242,000 killed

Name _____ Date _____

Earthquake Vocabulary

How well do you understand the following terms dealing with earthquakes? Below and to the left are a number of definitions. In the blank after each definition, write the word that is described by the definition. Use the terms given at the end of the exercise.

Definition	**Term**
1. The exterior solid part of the earth's surface	_____
2. Smaller quakes that come after a major earthquake	_____
3. Masses of snow sliding down a hill	_____
4. The edges of two of the earth's plates	_____
5. Melted rock	_____
6. The point on the surface of the earth located directly above the focus of the quake	_____
7. A famous fault that runs through California	_____
8. Located below the earth's surface, it is the point where the earthquake begins.	_____
9. The earthquake and volcano belt in countries that border the Pacific Ocean	_____
10. Small tremors before a major quake	_____
11. Size or extent of a particular earthquake	_____
12. The theory that holds that the continents of the world move a few inches every year	_____
13. A scientist who studies fossils in order to discover facts about prehistoric plants and creatures	_____
14. The measuring system invented by Dr. Charles F. Richter to gauge the strength of earthquakes	_____
15. To steal or rob	_____
16. Instruments that make a record of the time, duration, direction, and intensity of earthquakes	_____
17. A scientist who studies earthquakes	_____
18. Waves that go out from an earthquake's epicenter; they rock from side to side quickly.	_____
19. A large ocean wave caused by a seaquake or an earthquake	_____
20. A huge fire that does a great deal of damage	_____
21. Very hot rock located 1,800 miles deep beneath the crust	_____
22. Rising and falling in waves	_____
23. The impression of an animal or plant left in a rock deposit; sometimes the animal or plant is also found in the deposit.	_____

Name _____ Date _____

24. The layer of molten rock that covers the outer core of the center of _____
    the earth

25. The liquid layer of molten iron covering the inner core of the earth _____

26. One of several, moving sections on the earth's crust _____

27. A rapid shaking of the earth's surface _____

28. A scientist who studies the earth _____

29. Before recorded history _____

30. Masses of mud, dirt, and rock that slides down a hill _____

31. A person that studies the weather _____

32. A shaking of the earth _____

aftershocks, avalanche, conflagration, continental drift, crust, earthquake, epicenter, faults, focus, foreshocks, fossil, geologist, inner core, landslide, loot, magma, magnitude, mantle, meteorologist, outer core, paleontologist, plate, prehistoric, Richter scale, Ring of Fire, San Andreas fault, seismographs, seismologist, shock waves, tremors, tsunami, undulate

Identify the Layers of the Earth

Write the name of the correct layer of the earth on each line below.

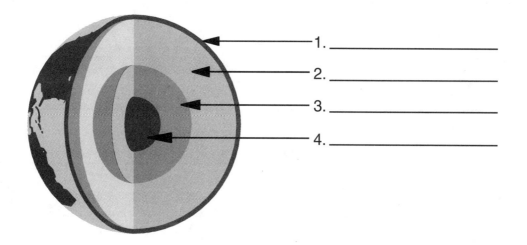

1. _____

2. _____

3. _____

4. _____

© Mark Twain Media, Inc., Publishers

Name _____ Date _____

Research and Thinking for Earthquakes

There are two scales used to describe the magnitude of an earthquake. The **Richter Scale**, which is better known than the other, shows the magnitude of an earthquake by the amount of energy released. Unlike the Richter Scale, the **Mercalli Scale** is based on intensity and ranges from 1 to 12 using Roman Numerals. The Mercalli Scale describes the intensity of an earthquake by observing the effects of an earthquake on people and property. Go to the library or do research on the Internet to find out more about the Mercalli scale. Then describe each magnitude level by using the chart below.

Mercalli Scale
Describe the Damage
I.
II.
III.
IV.
V.
VI.
VII.
VIII.
IX.
X.
XI.
XII.

© Mark Twain Media, Inc., Publishers

The Day the Mississippi Ran Backwards

THE NEW MADRID EARTHQUAKE OF 1811

When people think of earthquakes in the United States, most immediately think of San Francisco or Los Angeles, California. Both of these cities have experienced tremendous earthquakes. Not only have the quakes been strong and frequent, these two cities are heavily populated and have many tall buildings and a complicated and vast **infrastructure**. When an earthquake occurs at these locations, there is the potential for tremendous damage and loss of life. Few people are aware, however, that in 1811 the largest series of earthquakes to hit North America did not occur in California along the famous San Andreas fault, but in the Midwest at New Madrid, Missouri.

Located in the southeast corner of the state on the Mississippi River, New Madrid was named for **Madrid**, **Spain**. In the early part of the nineteenth century it was a prosperous community and considered an important landing between the Ohio River and **Natchez**, **Mississippi**. The people living in New Madrid were well aware of the dangers of living close to the river. Spring floods were a recurring part of life in New Madrid as it was in many towns located along the Mississippi.

But, as the citizens of New Madrid went to bed on the evening of December 15,1811, they were about to learn of another danger of living in this area. At a little after 2 a.m., a low rumbling began and grew in intensity. Dishes fell from tables and cabinets. Furniture crashed to the floor. Chimneys collapsed. Cabins and homes began to creak and groan with such intensity, the residents ran outside before their homes were destroyed. This was the first of several major shocks to hit the region throughout the winter. People talk about the New Madrid earthquake, but actually there were several major quakes and thousands of aftershocks that occurred through the winter of 1811–1812. Although the Richter Scale or the Mercalli Scale, used to measure the intensity of earthquakes, had not yet been invented, it has been estimated that these quakes would rank between 8.0 and 8.5 on the Richter Scale.

Abstract numbers cannot describe the power of these quakes, however. People who lived through them and wrote about what they saw have left a **vivid** description of the **awesome** power of this **natural disaster**. These descriptions

---

DISASTER AT A GLANCE

WHAT: The largest series of earthquakes in North America

WHERE: Along the Mississippi River, close to New Madrid, Missouri

WHEN: The winter of 1811–1812

© Mark Twain Media, Inc., Publishers

tell us that the earth actually rolled in waves, as if it were a lake and not land. Deep **crevasses** appeared and swallowed trees, horses, and cows. Long **fissures** several hundred feet long belched a foul sulphur odor and spewed out sand, water, and mud. Entire towns were destroyed.

Those who were on the Mississippi when the shocks and aftershocks hit had even more bizarre and terrifying stories. To some, it appeared as if the river sprang to life. Huge waves rocked and swamped boats. The water boiled and swirled. Fissures opened underneath the surface causing **whirlpools**. **Debris** shot through the surface as if shot from a cannon. In some spots, the river dropped several feet and falls were formed. Banks toppled into the river. Lakes were created. The *New Orleans,* a steamboat on its first voyage, reported they tied their boat to an island, but in the morning, the island had disappeared. It has been reported that the river was in such an agitated state, that for several hours it ran backwards.

The New Madrid Earthquake is remarkable because of its intensity, duration, and the area it affected. It was one of the most intense in North America. People living in St. Louis, Missouri, 200 miles away, were able to feel the shocks from the quake. In **Vicksburg,** Mississippi, large **sinkholes** were formed. In Kentucky, 120 miles from the epicenter, a clear spring became muddy for several hours. Buildings shook in **Raleigh**, North Carolina, and, in South Carolina, the air was filled with the smell of sulphur. As far away as Washington, D.C., it is reported that residents could feel the **tremors**. There have even been accounts of the quake causing bells to ring in Boston, Massachusetts. It has been estimated that the quake was felt in 28 states.

The length of the New Madrid Earthquake is also what makes it memorable. The series of quakes, which is generally referred to as the New Madrid Earthquake, lasted longer than any other quake in North American history. The shocks and aftershocks continued for about a year after the initial shock in December. The minor tremors became so frequent that many residents ignored them.

Another remarkable thing about the New Madrid Earthquake is the large area it affected. Earthquakes in the central and eastern United States do not occur as frequently as they do in the western United States, but they affect larger areas. The area of damage and destruction of earthquakes centered in the Midwest is much larger than in the west.

Will an earthquake hit the Midwest again? Experts tell us that it is not a question of *if* it will happen, it is a question of *when* it will happen. Moderate to severe earthquakes occur in the Midwest about once every 80 years. The last quake of this magnitude was in 1895. The probability of a moderate earthquake occurring in the New Madrid area in the near future is high. Experts predict that there is a 50 percent chance of the moderate quake occurring by the year 2000 and a 90 percent chance of one occurring by 2040. Such an earthquake could hit the **Mississippi Valley** at any time.

What makes this worrisome is that the region is more heavily populated than it was in 1811. Also, since earthquakes happen so infrequently in this area, most buildings that would be affected were not built to withstand the stress of a severe quake. In Japan and California, where quakes are more frequent, builders design structures that will not collapse during a quake.

Name _____ · _____ Date _____

Checking What You Have Read—The New Madrid Quake

Complete the following statements below with information from the narrative about the New Madrid quake.

1. The largest series of earthquakes to hit North America occurred at _____.

2. New Madrid, Missouri, is located on the banks of the _____.

3. New Madrid, Missouri, is named after _____.

4. The New Madrid Earthquake of 1811 was not just one quake, it was a _____ of quakes.

5. The New Madrid Earthquake of 1811 was memorable not only because of its intensity, but because of its _____.

6. Earthquakes often disrupt facilities and services such as transportation, communication, water, and power lines. These elements help make up the _____ of a community.

7. Experts predict that there is a_____ percent chance of the moderate quake occurring along the New Madrid fault by the year 2000.

8. Earthquakes in the central and eastern United States do not occur as frequently as they do in the western United States, but they affect _____ areas.

9. Experts predict that there is a_____ percent chance of a moderate quake occurring along the New Madrid fault by the year 2040.

10. During the New Madrid quake of 1811, the river was in such an agitated state, that for several hours it ran_____.

11. The shocks and aftershocks continued for about a _____ after the initial shock in December.

12. The quake caused bells to ring in_____.

13. Moderate to severe earthquakes occur in the Midwest about once every _____ years.

14. In the early part of the nineteenth century, New Madrid was an important landing between the _____ and _____.

15. The series of New Madrid Earthquakes began on_____.

16. The New Madrid quake was felt in_____ states.

17. Two large California cities that are known for earthquakes are _____ and _____.

18. The last moderate quake to hit the Midwest occurred in_____.

19. In Vicksburg, Mississippi, large_____ were formed during the quake.

20. A foreign country that has frequent quakes and has designed buildings to survive these quakes is _____.

21. In Kentucky, a clear spring became _____ for several hours.

22. Long fissures several hundred feet long belched a foul _____ odor during the quake.

23. The intensity of the New Madrid Earthquake was estimated at_____ on the Richter Scale.

24. New Madrid, Missouri, is located in the _____ corner of the state.

The Day the Earth Danced
SAN FRANCISCO QUAKE OF 1906

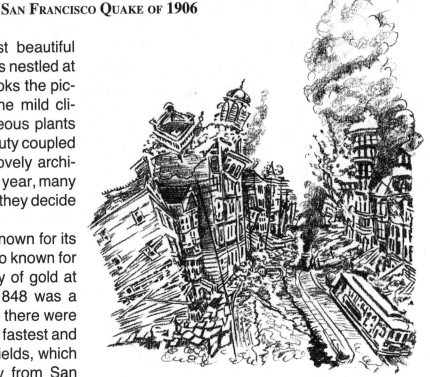

Known as one of the most beautiful cities in America, San Francisco is nestled at the foot of mountains and overlooks the picturesque San Francisco Bay. The mild climate encourages lush and gorgeous plants and flowers. All of this natural beauty coupled with unique and extraordinarily lovely architecture entices many visitors each year, many of whom find the city so charming they decide to make it their home.

Not only is San Francisco known for its beauty and its setting, but it is also known for its colorful history. The discovery of gold at Sutter's Creek in California in 1848 was a blessing to San Francisco. Since there were no transcontinental railroads, the fastest and cheapest way to get to the gold fields, which were less than 100 miles away from San Francisco, was by sea. Therefore, almost everyone and everything heading for the gold fields passed through this busy seaport.

It wasn't only the gold rush that made San Francisco a busy port. San Francisco Bay is the largest of the very few bays along the California coastline. A safe harbor protecting ships from Asia and Europe was the biggest asset a city could have. It not only guaranteed that a large city would be built in this location, it practically assured its success. And San Francisco was successful. It grew and flourished. Immigrants from around the world came to this prosperous city not only to work, but also to become entrepreneurs and, ultimately, become wealthy themselves.

San Francisco grew. Its population increased from just a few hundred before the discovery of gold to over one-half million by 1906. This rapid growth encouraged builders to quickly erect buildings in order to accommodate the businesses and residents of this thriving community. Since it was faster and cheaper to erect wooden buildings, most were constructed this way. While these buildings were not as sturdy, not as safe, and were prone to burn, not many people worried. After all, the city and its citizens were doing well.

There was one problem with this successful, modern city, however. The site, which was so beautiful and so strategically located for commerce, was right on top of what is known as the San Andreas fault. A **fault** is a fracture in the earth's crust where two tectonic plates meet. The San Andreas fault, which is about 600 miles long and reaches from the Gulf of California to north of San Francisco, marks the separation of the North American

---

DISASTER AT A GLANCE

WHAT: One of the most significant earthquakes in American history

WHERE: San Francisco, California

WHEN: April 18, 1906

WHY: The San Andreas fault ruptured, causing a quake that was 7.7–7.9 on the Richter scale.

DEATHS: At least 850 people killed, 225,000 left homeless, and 28,000 buildings destroyed

COST: $400 million in 1906 dollars

AFTERMATH: Technical advances in construction of buildings and infrastructure are implemented to save lives, reduce fires, and keep buildings from collapsing.

---

and Pacific tectonic plates. These plates actually float and move or drift on the earth's mantle, which is composed of melted rock. When these plates collide with each other, or when they suddenly pull apart, an earthquake occurs.

In 1906, the citizens of San Francisco did not know about tectonic plates, nor the San Andreas Fault. It wasn't until 1912 that a German scientist named Alfred Wegener developed the theory of tectonic plates and continental drift. San Fransciscans were aware that California had more earthquakes than other states. Minor quakes were frequent. In fact, there was a major earthquake in San Francisco in 1808, but since the city was sparsely populated, the effects of the quake were not devastating. So the citizens of this beautiful community were not worried. That is, until 5:13 a.m. on April 18, 1906.

The 500,000 inhabitants of San Francisco were jolted awake that morning with a foreshock that was felt throughout the area. About 25 seconds later, the earthquake began. The earth began to undulate violently. The quake lasted less than a minute, but the damage was horrendous. Streets were split open, smoke stacks fell, and pipes burst. Some buildings collapsed, but most did not. However, the substandard construction practices designed to save money left most buildings damaged so severely they were dangerous to be in. Foundations were cracked, and they tilted precariously. And worst of all, the wooden construction, favored for putting up buildings quickly and cheaply, would turn out not to be such a bargain after all.

Although the quake had caused tremendous damage, there was even more bad news to come. The quake had broken gas pipes, and the leaking gas was ignited by downed power lines, causing many fires within minutes of the initial shock. The fires burned out of control, decimating the city. At first, fire fighters did not respond to the fires. The quake had broken the batteries that powered the fire alarm system. Fire fighters eventually raced to the blazes but were unable to do much to stop the fires. The quake had also broken the city's water pipes. The fire fighters tried to use the water in cisterns. **Cisterns** were storage tanks or basins located underground that designed to catch and keep rainwater, but these were also dry. In desperation, the fire fighters tried to contain the fire by creating firebreaks. They blew up buildings and streets with explosives, but by and large, they were unsuccessful, and in some cases, even started other blazes.

The fire raged for many days. It began on Wednesday morning, and by Saturday it was out. When the smoke finally cleared, the survivors could finally see the extent of the damage. Nearly five square miles of the city had been burned. Originally it was reported that 450 died. More recently the figure was set at 800. One study even suggested that more that 3,000 people lost their lives either directly or indirectly as a result of this disaster. Another 300,000 were left homeless—that was more than 50 percent of the city's population. The property damage was also enormous. Over 28,000 buildings were destroyed. The estimated property damage has been set at $400,000,000. And that is in 1906 dollars.

Today, San Francisco is rebuilt and has grown tremendously. If an earthquake of the intensity of the 1906 quake occurred today, what would happen? We have learned a lot from this and other quakes. Modern buildings are designed to resist quakes and not collapse. Power lines now have circuit breakers that stop the current to broken lines. There are automatic shut-off valves on gas lines. Water mains are built to resist the movement of the earth. Emergency broadcasts warn citizens of fires, floods, and damaged bridges. Fire fighters also have more powerful and sophisticated tools to stop fires.

In spite of all this, our cities are more densely populated than in 1906, and a quake the size of the one in 1906 would be very costly in human, as well as economic, terms. There would probably be tens of thousands of people killed and many more injured. The economic damage would also be great. There would probably be billions of dollars in damage, even though buildings are built sturdier today and are designed to withstand earthquakes.

Name_____ Date _____

California and the San Andreas Fault

Using an atlas, find the following locations on the map below: **San Diego, Los Angles, San Andreas fault, Sacramento, San Jose, San Francisco, San Francisco Bay, Sutter's Mill.** On the line next to each number below, write the name of the location.

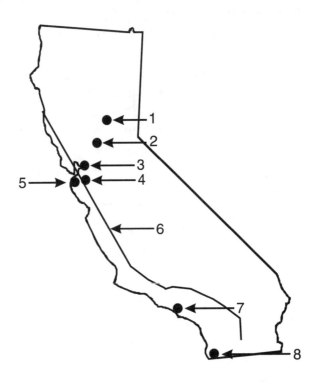

1. _____

2. _____

3. _____

4. _____

5. _____

6. _____

7. _____

8. _____

© Mark Twain Media, Inc., Publishers

Name _____ Date _____

How Are Earthquakes Measured?

1. Here is a picture of instruments used to measure earthquakes. Identify the instruments and, in your own words,
   explain how they work.

_____

_____

_____

_____

_____

_____

2. There are two scales used to measure the intensity of an earthquake. Name each and, in your
   own words, describe how they work.

_____

_____

_____

_____

3. Ancient people had some bizarre notions to explain earthquakes. What are some?

_____

_____

_____

_____

4. Some people believe that animals can predict earthquakes. Do you think this is possible? If so,
   why?

_____

_____

_____

_____

© Mark Twain Media, Inc., Publishers   61

Name_____ Date _____

Surviving an Earthquake

In the spaces listed below, develop a plan to survive an earthquake.

1. What should I do to prepare in case of an earthquake?

_____

_____

_____

2. If I am indoors when a quake occurs, here is what I should do to survive.

_____

_____

_____

_____

3. If I am outdoors when a quake occurs, here is what I should do to survive.

_____

_____

_____

_____

4. After a quake, here is what I should do.

_____

_____

_____

_____

_____

© Mark Twain Media, Inc., Publishers

Name _____ Date _____

Improving Your Vocabulary

Read each of the following sentences that have been adapted from the information on the San Francisco Earthquake. Below each sentence are four words. One of these words is a synonym for the word that is in bold print. Circle the word that most nearly matches, and write a sentence of your own that uses the word in bold type.

1. San Francisco is **nestled** at the foot of mountains.
   A. low   B. found   C. sheltered   D. built

   _____

2. San Francisco overlooks the **picturesque** San Francisco Bay.
   A. familiar   B. striking   C. unrealistic   D. ancient

   _____

3. The mild climate encourages **lush** and gorgeous plants and flowers.
   A. abundant   B. meager   C. pretty   D. attractive

   _____

4. All of this natural beauty is coupled with **unique** and extraordinary architecture.
   A. ornamental   B. large   C. beautiful   D. unequalled

   _____

5. This natural beauty **entices** many visitors.
   A. mystifies   B. lures   C. amuses   D. charms

   _____

6. A safe harbor was the biggest **asset** a city could have.
   A. shelter   B. port   C. value   D. liability

   _____

7. Immigrants from around the world came to this **prosperous** city.
   A. flourishing   B. international   C. large   D. friendly

   _____

8. Immigrants became **entrepreneurs**.
   A. sailors   B. miners   C. businessmen   D. builders

   _____

9. San Francisco **flourished**.
   A. collapsed   B. buckled   C. died   D. grew

   _____

10. Builders quickly erected buildings in this **thriving** community.
    A. prosperous   B. decadent   C. deteriorating   D. carefree

    _____

11. The location was beautiful and **strategically** located.
    A. solidly   B. unsatisfactory C. miserably   D. essentially

    _____

© Mark Twain Media, Inc., Publishers   63

Name _____ Date _____

12. The location was good for **commerce**.

    A. ships   B. business   C. trains   D. builders

13. In 1808, the city was **sparsely** populated.

    A. heavily   B. densely   C. meagerly   D. luxuriously

14. The effects of the quake were **devastating**.

    A. overwhelming   B. recorded   C. concentrated   D. hallowed

15. The earth began to **undulate** violently.

    A. spin   B. whirl   C. wave   D. deviate

16. The quake lasted less than a minute, but the damage was **horrendous**.

    A. concentrated   B. hasty   C. terrible   D. interesting

17. The **substandard** construction practices were designed to save money.

    A. underground   B. underwater   C. quality   D. inferior

18. Foundations were cracked, and they tilted **precariously**.

    A. listing   B. comically   C. dangerously   D. lopsided

19. The fires burned out of control, **decimating** the city.

    A. destroying   B. building   C. multiplying   D. burgeoning

20. The fire fighters tried to use the water in **cisterns**.

    A. tanks   B. hoses   C. hydrants   D. bay

21. The fire **raged** for many days.

    A. simmered   B. lasted   C. flared   D. smoldered

22. Our cities are more **densely** populated.

    A. meagerly   B. sparsely   C. heavily   D. desirably

23. These buildings were **prone** to burn.

    A. impossible   B. burgeoned   C. unlikely   D. susceptible

© Mark Twain Media, Inc., Publishers

Risking Death for $9 a Week
THE TRIANGLE SHIRTWAIST CO. FIRE

It was nearly quitting time on Saturday, March 25, 1911, and Sophie Klein and her fellow workers at the Triangle Shirtwaist Company were getting ready to go home. Most of the workers in the factory were German, Yiddish, and Italian immigrant "girls." The term "girls" was not just a demeaning term, it was, in fact, accurate. Many of the workers were less than 20 years old. Sophie was one of the younger girls at 15. Today she was tired. She generally worked from 7:30 a.m. until 6 p.m., but when the company was busy, her boss told her she had to work until 9 p.m. If she refused, she would be fired. Sometimes she was told she also had to work on Saturday and Sunday if she wanted to keep her job. There was a sign on the bulletin board at the entrance to the factory that said, "If you don't come in on Sunday, don't come in on Monday."

There were only two good things Sophie liked about the extra work. First, there was a bigger paycheck. While she did not get extra pay for longer hours or weekend work, the extra hours brought her weekly pay up to almost $9. The second good thing about weekend work was the earlier quitting time on Saturday and Sunday. At 4:45 p.m. her day was over.

Sohpie's thoughts were interrupted by a voice that shouted, "Fire!" At first she thought it was a joke. After all, the 10-story Asch Building, which housed the Triangle Shirtwaist Company, was of the most modern construction and considered fireproof. It was made of brick and concrete and could hardly burn down. In fact, the building had experienced four fires recently without major damage. But then Sophie smelled the smoke.

Sophie ran to the only fire escape. It was hard to get through the maze of sewing machines that were placed close together, but she finally made it. When she tried the door to the fire escape, though, she found it was locked. The owners kept all of the doors locked so that the workers couldn't steal anything. As Sophie struggled to force the door open, a great crowd of workers pressed her from behind. The crowd became hysterical. They screamed, pushed, and shoved in an effort to escape. Finally, someone picked up the head of a sewing machine and smashed it against the top part of the door, which was made of thick, frosted glass. The glass shattered, and Sophie and many others climbed through the broken pane and ran downstairs and out into the street.

When Sophie got outside, she could see that she was one of the lucky ones. Dead bodies of workers littered the sidewalk. Many were workers who had jumped to their deaths rather than be burned alive. There were others who had hung by their hands and then were forced to let go when the fire burned their hands. One girl jumped from the ninth floor and would have immediately smashed into the pavement, but her clothing caught on a hook that stuck out from the wall on the eighth floor. Eventually, however, the fire burned through her clothing, and she fell to her death. Another girl fell from the eighth floor, but at the sixth floor, a hook from a sign caught her clothes and held her. She was

---

DISASTER AT A GLANCE

WHAT: The Triangle Shirtwaist Co. Fire

WHERE: New York City

WHEN: March 25, 1911

WHY: No fire safety; exit doors were locked

DEATHS: 146

AFTERMATH: Several labor laws designed to protect workers were enacted. It also helped increase support for unions to organize workers in the garment district.

able to break a window on the sixth floor, crawl into the building, and escape to the street.

By this time, the fire department had arrived. The firemen had to be careful as they moved their rigging into place because of the many bodies that were scattered on the street and sidewalk. As they began to raise their ladders and turn on their hoses, more bodies crashed down on them. Several fireman held a fire net to catch a girl who was ready to jump from the ninth story window. She jumped and hit the net, but immediately afterward, three others jumped on top of her. The net broke and all four were killed.

When the fireman finally set up their apparatus, they realized that the stream of water from their hoses would only reach the seventh floor—one floor short of the fire. To make matters worse, their ladders only reached between the sixth and seventh floors. They could not use the ladders to rescue those who were trapped. Several girls on the eighth floor jumped for the ladder that was extended two stories below. They all missed and crashed to their deaths.

Inside the building on the eighth floor, where the fire began, the flames grew more intense as it was fueled by cotton cloth. Some of the male workers desperately tried to put the fire out with the available water buckets, but it was no use. The fire escape that Sophie had used collapsed, killing several people and eliminating an escape route for those who were still trapped.

Many girls raced for the elevators and the stairway. Unfortunately, the doors to the stairway opened in rather than out, so the workers trying to escape actually pushed the door closed. The constant pressure from the mob made it impossible for those in front to pull the doors open.

Some of the workers acted heroically to save their fellow workers. The elevator operators brought the two elevators to the eighth floor. Although the elevators were built to hold only 10 passengers, they were able to pack in almost 15. Each elevator made several trips bringing the hysterical and badly burned girls to safety. Some workers could not wait for their turn on the

elevator, however, and tried to slide down on elevator cables. They lost their grip and were killed. Upstairs, three male workers tried to save some of the girls by forming a human chain from an eighth floor window to the window of the building next door. Several girls were able to climb over on the backs of the three, but the men lost their balance, and all three fell to their deaths in the street below.

Because of the magnitude of the fire, it is hard to believe that it only lasted about one-half hour and was confined to only the eighth, ninth, and tenth floors of the building. Of the 600 employes of the shirtwaist company, 146 were killed. When the firemen were finally able to enter the building, they were appalled at the grotesque scene. The bodies were burned and charred so badly, they did not even look human. There were 19 bodies melted against the locked door. Twenty-five bodies were found in a cloakroom trying to hide from the inferno. Another 25 scorched bodies were found on top of the elevator.

No one ever discovered how the fire started. There is a theory that one of the men threw a match or cigarette onto the floor, which was cluttered with cloth scraps. The reason the fire spread so quickly was the abundance of cloth. Ironically, the fireproof building showed little damage. Only the cloth and the people inside were affected.

Issac Harris and Max Blanck, owners of the Triangle Company, went to trial for manslaughter. The main charge was that they kept the doors locked, so it was impossible for the workers to escape during the fire. They were acquitted by a New York jury. Several families of the victims sued the two owners, and eventually each family was paid $75.

As a result of the fire, several labor laws designed to protect workers were enacted. Among them:

- All doors must open outwards.
- Doors are not to be locked during working hours.
- Sprinkler systems are required for companies employing more than 25 people above the ground floor.
- Fire drills are mandatory for buildings without sprinkler systems.

The fire was also important in that it helped increase support for unions to organize workers in the garment district and especially for the International Ladies' Garment Workers' Union. Even today, The Triangle Shirtwaist Co. Fire is a symbol for the American labor movement and the need for the government to ensure a safe workplace.

After the fire, the International Ladies' Garment Workers' Union proposed that the city hold an official day of mourning.

Name _____ Date _____

Research and Thinking For the Triangle Shirtwaist Co. Fire

1. Issac Harris and Max Blanck, owners of the Triangle Company, went to trial for manslaughter, but were not convicted. Do you agree with this verdict? Write down specific reasons for your decision.

_____

_____

_____

_____

_____

2. If you think the two owners should have been found guilty, why do you suppose they were not?

_____

_____

_____

3. Many of the fire disasters in the United States have resulted in laws that have improved safety standards. Using the Internet or the library, list other famous fires in the United States that have resulted in improved fire safety. Here are some links you might want to begin with: Twentieth Century U.S. Fire Disasters, fire in the United States, fire safety, and fire protection.

_____

_____

_____

4. We tend to believe that sweatshops no longer exist. This is not true. Using the Internet or the library, list more modern examples of sweatshops.

_____

_____

_____

_____

Floods

It you were to look at an atlas, you would find most major cities are located close to bodies of water. This is not a coincidence. **Oceans**, **rivers**, and **lakes** offer many advantages for settlements. **Marine** life offers a wide range of food and occupations for people living nearby. **Transportation** is another advantage of living near a waterway. Shipping is an efficient way to transport goods and supplies to and from other cities and countries. Farmers also benefit by living close to waterways. Rivers, for example, often flood and leave rich **silt** along the banks when the river recedes. This silt is very **fertile** and is ideal for farming. You may have read how Egyptians developed their culture thousands of years ago by farming the rich delta soil of the **Nile**. Each year, the Nile River would overflow, leaving rich **alluvial** soil when the floodwaters receded.

In spite of the many advantages of living close to a body of water, there is one major disadvantage—**flooding**. The most common type of flooding occurs along rivers and streams. Heavy rains and rapid snow melt causes a large amount of water to flow, filling not only the natural **channel** of the river or **riverbed,** but also overflowing the banks into the low areas near the channel. This is called the **flood plain**.

People who have settled near a river often take steps to protect their communities, farms, and homes by building **levees**, which are hills of earth that raise the banks so that the river does not flow into the flood plain. Other communities build **dams** to control the flow of the river. A lake or **reservoir** is formed behind the dam. The lake can provide a water supply, **irrigation**, or recreation for the nearby community. It may also provide electricity, or its purpose may be just to control the flow of the water. If there is little rain or the river is low, the **outlet** of the dam may be closed or opened only slightly. When there is a great deal of rain and the water in the river is high, the outlet of the dam may be opened wider. If the flow of the water is too great to be discharged through the **outlet**, there is a safety valve called a **spillway** that allows the water to leave the reservoir so the dam is not damaged.

Since dams hold back so much water and are under constant pressure, dams are constantly being inspected and maintained, to ensure they remain strong and able to perform the job for which they were built. One of the worst floods in our history occurred in 1889 in Johnstown, Pennsylvania, when a dam broke and caused a **flash flood**. Fortunately, most dams are strong, and the chance they will break is very small.

Flash floods are not only caused by dams breaking. A sudden, heavy rain can cause a river to overflow its banks or a levee to be breached very quickly. Flash floods are the kind of floods that cause the most deaths. Since they occur quickly, without warning, people are often unprepared. Flash floods happen most frequently in mountainous areas, and the water flows with such force that trees, cars, and people are easily swept away.

In the United States, the **Mississippi River**, one of the longest rivers of North America, causes frequent flooding. Other areas prone to flooding include the central valley of California and the Missouri and Arkansas River **basins**. Flooding along **coastlines** is also a concern. **Hurricanes** are responsible for most of the flooding in these areas. Hurricanes can cause flooding in two ways. First, strong winds and high ocean tides or **storm surges** cause flooding along the coast as the strong waves created by a hurricane pound the beaches, eroding the natural barriers or **buffers** that protect the community homes and roads from the sea. Second, the hurricanes cause heavy rain that not only causes flooding along the coast, but can also cause flooding, especially flash floods, hundreds of miles **inland**.

Another kind of flooding is caused by a **tsunami**. Tsunamis are caused by underwater earthquakes or volcanic eruptions. Most tsunamis have occurred on the islands and in the countries that border the Pacific Ocean. The mainland United States, Alaska, and Hawaii have experienced tsunamis. Japan is particularly susceptible to tsunamis.

© Mark Twain Media, Inc., Publishers

Name _____ Date _____

Flood Vocabulary

How well do you understand the following terms dealing with floods? Below and to the left are a number of definitions. In the blank after each definition, write the word that is described. Use the terms given below.

Definition	**Term**
1. Egyptians farmed in the rich delta soil of this river.	_____
2. Organisms that live in the sea	_____
3. A sediment deposited by floods	_____
4. A huge body of salt water	_____
5. A triangular alluvial deposit at the mouth of a river	_____
6. A large stream of water that empties into an ocean or lake	_____
7. The business of moving passengers or goods	_____
8. When water overflows into an area that is normally dry	_____
9. Name given to soil that is rich and that grows crops easily	_____
10. A large inland body of water	_____
11. The natural channel through which a river flows	_____
12. A low area that surrounds a river bank and is frequently flooded	_____
13. A safety valve to drain excess water from dams	_____
14. Wall of earth that raises the banks of a river to prevent flooding	_____
15. A barrier built to restrict the flow of water	_____
16. The part of the dam through which water is usually discharged	_____
17. A sudden and forceful flood	_____
18. To artificially supply dry areas with water	_____
19. A lake used to store and regulate the flow of water	_____
20. One of the longest rivers of North America	_____
21. An area drained by a specific river system	_____
22. A huge wave caused by an underwater earthquake	_____
23. Something that protects or absorbs the shock of an impact	_____
24. The interior of a country	_____
25. The area of the country along the ocean	_____
26. A tropical cyclone	_____

basin, buffer, coastline, dam, delta, fertile, flash flood, flooding, flood plain, hurricane, inland, irrigate, lake, levee, marine, Mississippi, Nile, ocean, outlet, reservoir, river, riverbed, silt, spillway, transportation, tsunami

The Raging Mississippi

The Mississippi River begins in Minnesota and snakes its way down the middle of the United States before it empties into the Gulf of Mexico. The name Mississippi is taken from a Native American word and literally means "big river." Since the Mississippi drains most of the territory between the Rocky and Allegheny mountains, flooding is common along its main channel and its tributaries. There have been many significant and destructive floods along this river. Even before European explorers came, the Indians were aware of the devastation possible by the Mississippi. Tribes who lived close to the river built their homes on high ground to avoid damage from the river's frequent flooding.

De Soto Expedition: 1539

One of the first white explorers to experience the intensity of the flooding Mississippi was Hernando de Soto, a Spanish explorer who came to America to search for gold in 1539. He and his men arrived at the Mississippi in the spring, and as they began building boats on the banks of the mighty river, it began to rise. Since there were no levees at this time, the area in which they were working flooded. This was no great problem, they just decided to move their work to higher ground. But the rain continued, and the river began to rise, flooding them out again. The explorers were unaware they

were working in a floodplain. This is one of many flat, low-lying areas by the river that flood frequently. The Mississippi floodplain often stretches from the river to cliffs or bluffs miles away.

De Soto's men were surprised when the river overflowed its banks. They were more surprised when the rain continued for several weeks and the water completely filled the floodplain. They were astonished when the river continued its rise and finally reached the top of the cliffs and then went over the cliffs to the land much higher than the river.

The Flood of 1927—Arkansas

When settlers first began to live and farm close to the Mississippi, they began to build levees to protect their land, homes, and communities. During a normal year, they were able to withstand the rising water caused by heavy rains. Their communities grew, and more and more people settled along the banks of this mighty river. The spring of 1927, however, was to be different. Actually, the heavy rainfall in the area that drains into the Mississippi began in 1926 and continued through the spring of 1927. This unusually long downpour had two effects. First, it raised the level of the river to record crests. Second, the levees and dikes that were placed along the banks to protect the communities and farms became saturated and weak. If this were not bad enough, the weather turned warm, melting snow in the north. This caused a torrent of water to swirl down the river and attack the already weakened levees.

There was just too much water and too much power to contain the river. A break or breach occurred at Mount Landing, Arkansas, in April 1927. Workers tried to repair the break, but the rushing water was too strong. Within minutes, the break was about one mile wide. Several other levees broke, and farms, homes, and in some cases, entire communities were swallowed up by the raging water. Eventually, the flood waters spread over several states. Arkansas, Louisiana, and Mississippi were affected the most. Over 300 people died as a result of this flood. Over 500,000 people lost their homes, and the damage has been estimated at more than $300 million.

THE FLOOD OF 1937

The great flood of 1927 encouraged Congress to improve the levee system along the Mississippi so that a flood of that magnitude could never happen again. They passed the Flood Control Act in 1928 that appropriated $325 million to add and improve levees along the Mississippi River, as well as to regulate the flow of water. The organization selected for the job was the U.S. Army Corps of Engineers. In addition to improving the levees, they also cleared the channel of snags and dredged it to a minimum depth of nine feet. Additional money has been appropriated to the Corps over the years, and they have improved the safety of the river and minimized the flooding. However, they were unable to do much as heavy rains that soaked the Ohio Valley swelled the Ohio River to above flood stage, in January 1937. The Ohio River is a main tributary of the Mississippi, and when it flowed to meet the mighty Mississippi at Cairo, Illinois, the amount of water from both rivers caused the river to rise dramatically.

The levee at Cairo did hold, but the U.S. Army Corps of Engineers knew that it would not be able to hold forever, so they made a spillway by dynamiting along the river's bank. The engineers and volunteers worked frantically along the levees south of Cairo. One main concern was that New Orleans is located in a very low area, and if its levees were breached, the city could be under water. In a desperate effort to divert some of the water that would flow to New Orleans and perhaps breach its levees, a spillway was opened just to the north of New Orleans. The water from the spillway was drained into Lake Pontchartrain. New Orleans was saved. But there were still 137 deaths because of the flood, and the rushing water destroyed more than 13,000 homes.

© Mark Twain Media, Inc., Publishers   72

Name _____ Date _____

Checking What You Have Read

Based upon what you read in the section entitled, "The Raging Mississippi," fill in the appropriate word or words in the following sentences.

1. One of the first white explorers to explore the Mississippi was _____.

2. This explorer came from _____ .

3. He came to America to find _____.

4. He arrived at the Mississippi River in the spring of_____.

5. A _____ is a wall of earth built so that a river will not overflow its banks.

6. Cliffs along the river are often called _____.

7. The_____ River begins in Minnesota and flows south down the middle of the United States.

8. This river empties into the _____ .

9. The Mississippi River drains most of the territory between the_____ and _____ Mountains.

10. The name Mississippi is taken from a Native American word and literally means _____ _____.

11. A _____ is a stream or river that flows into a larger stream or river.

12. Another word for a break in a levee is a_____.

13. A break occurred at _____ in April 1927.

14. Spring floods are often caused by heavy spring_____ and melting _____.

15. The three states most affected by the Mississippi flood of 1927 were_____, _____ , and _____.

16. Over _____ people died as a result of the 1927 flood.

17. Damage from the 1927 flood is estimated at more than _____ dollars.

18. Over _____ people lost their homes as a result of the 1927 flood.

19. The great flood of 1927 encouraged Congress to pass _____.

20. Along with this act, Congress appropriated _____ dollars to add and improve levees along the Mississippi River.

21. The organization selected to improve and maintain the levees and river was the _____ _____.

22. The Corps of Engineers dredged the river to a minimum depth of _____ feet.

23. One of the causes of the Flood of 1937 was heavy rains in the _____ Valley.

24. The Ohio River is a main _____ of the Mississippi River.

25. In an effort to save New Orleans, a spillway was opened, and the water drained into _____ _____.

And a Great Flood Covered the Land
THE MID-AMERICA FLOOD OF 1993

In 1993, many communities along the Mississippi learned a horrible truth: All the money, technology, and volunteers in the world cannot control the Mississippi. People living next to this river had seen the river flood before. In 1927, 1937, 1965, and 1973 the river had toppled levees and caused millions of dollars worth of damage. It was hoped that, with improved forecasting, communication, and technology future floods could be minimized or even averted. So, many were not prepared when they experienced a flood that has gone down in history as one of the greatest disasters of the Midwest.

Much of Jefferson City, Missouri, was covered by flood waters from the Missouri River in 1993.

The Mississippi Valley had experienced a record rainfall for several weeks during the early summer of 1993. The rain was so heavy that, not only was the Mississippi above flood stage, so were the Des Moines, Iowa, Illinois, Minnesota, and Missouri Rivers. All of these are tributaries that empty into the Mississippi. The U.S. Corps of Engineers and thousands of volunteers fought the river, which rose by the hour.

Communities along the Mississippi sounded the alert, and thousands of volunteers did what they could to help save the levees. In most cases, a central location, such as an athletic field, was chosen, and volunteers of all ages met at this spot to fill sandbags to be used on the levees. Senior citizens worked alongside of elementary students. Rich worked along with poor. Whole families volunteered. Some made food for the volunteers. Others worked on the levees, checking for leaks or shoring up the levee with the sandbags. In some cases, even convicts from work farms or county jails joined in the battle. This volunteer spirit is one of the good things to come out of the disaster. For some, the communities' efforts paid off and the levee protecting the town was saved. But for many, the heroic efforts of the citizens could not stop the relentless assault of the river. One by one, the levees began to give away.

When levees were breached, so was access to the other side of the river. If it were flooded on one side of the river, people were unable to use the bridge to travel across the river. The high water also made some bridges just too dangerous to use. This made it especially difficult for people who lived on one side of the river and worked on the other. In some cases, so many bridges were closed that people who usually spent 20 minutes to cross a bridge and go to work, needed to travel miles to find a bridge open. It might take them three or four hours to make that same trip. Some merely rented an apartment close to work and only went home on weekends. Some people would take a boat to cross the river in the morning to go to work, and then take a boat to get home in the evening. Once the water began to recede, the bridges were still closed because water, mud, and debris covered the roads.

© Mark Twain Media, Inc., Publishers   74

One of the differences between the flood of 1993 and previous floods was the improved communications that enabled the world to witness the devastation on television each evening. It was a dramatic story as national news reporters interviewed people and video taped the scenes before the levees were breached and as the water was bursting through the earthen dams and dikes. The national news crews would follow the crest of the river and see how the citizens were coping with the disaster. One day the crews would be in Des Moines, Iowa, showing the flood. A few days later they would be Quincy, Illinois, and Hannibal, Missouri. A week later they would be in Cape Girardeau, Missouri.

Many communities received major damage. In Des Moines, Iowa, the city's water treatment plant was flooded. There was no safe water available in the city for twelve days. Ironically, many of the cities who also suffered from the flood sent drinking water to the citizens of Des Moines. In another community, the force of the cascading water dug up a cemetery and sent caskets floating downstream. Most were recovered and reburied, but some were never found.

Not only were homes lost, but so were schools. As school began in August, many students could not go back as they always had, because there was no school left. There were no books, no desks, no classrooms—nothing. Classes were set up in vacant buildings and other locations. This might seem like fun to some, but consider, with no gymnasium the sports teams either could not compete, or at least were unable to practice. The fun extracurricular activities such as dances, proms, sports, and clubs were either cancelled or modified so much many didn't bother to participate.

While many communities received major flood damage, some were completely devastated. Entire towns, such as Hull, Kaskaskia, Meyer, Niota, and Valmeyer, all in Illinois, were completely underwater. News crews in airplanes showed these and other towns, looking like a sea where the map said a town should be. Scattered throughout this sea were the tops of roofs that looked like small islands.

One of the tragedies of the flood was how it affected people. On the one hand, it brought people together to fight the flood. On the other hand, thousands of people lost their jobs. Manufacturers, restaurants, service stations, and others were destroyed. While some rebuilt, others did not. They felt they had enough of the floodplain, so they relocated. Farmers not only lost their entire crop for the year, some even were unable to plant the following spring. Before they could farm again, some needed to help rebuild private levees, clean their fields, and repair their homes, buildings, and equipment.

Sadly, it was learned that some of the levee breaks were not caused by faulty levees or the water just going over the top. Some of the levees were sabotaged. In some cases, people intentionally removed sand bags from the top of the levee so that the river would flood an area. This is what happened in West Quincy, Missouri, where thousands of acres of farmland were flooded, many businesses were destroyed, and the only bridge that had been open for several miles on the Mississippi was closed. The person responsible for this catastrophe was caught, tried, convicted, and sentenced to life in prison for causing a catastrophe.

On December 3, 1993, President Clinton signed a relief bill that appropriated $110 million to buy land from the residents who lived along the floodplain and turn it into wetlands or parks. The idea was to help people move from the floodplain, where flooding is always a danger. However, some decided that although they had lost everything, this was their home and moving to another community was simply out of the question.

While there were few deaths that could be attributed to the Great Flood of 1993, property damaged was estimated in the billions of dollars. However, the cost of this great flood is not tabulated just in dollars and cents, but rather in human suffering.

© Mark Twain Media, Inc., Publishers

Name _____ Date _____

How Well Do You Know the Mississippi?

Using the library or the Internet, find the answer to the following questions about the Mississippi River.

1. What is the length of the Mississippi? _____

2. How deep is the deepest point on the Mississippi?_____

3. How shallow is the shallowest point on the Mississippi? _____

4. What is the source? (where the Mississippi begins) _____

5. What is the outflow? (where the Mississippi ends) _____

6. Name three major tributaries of the Mississippi. _____

_____

7. Who were the first Europeans to see the Mississippi?_____

8. What is the name of the French explorer who claimed the river for France in 1682?

_____

9. What were the names of the French-Canadian explorer and the Jesuit missionary who opened the area to European influence? _____

10. How did the United States acquire the Mississippi River from France?_____

_____

11. Name the two explorers who, in 1804, headed an expedition to investigate the territory between the Mississippi River and the Pacific Ocean. _____

12. Name the states for which the Mississippi acts as a border. _____

_____

_____

13. Name some principal cities located on the Mississippi._____

_____

14. The Mississippi River is the second longest river in the United States. What is the longest?

_____

15. What Indian tribes have lived along the Mississippi?_____

_____

_____

Famous Rivers

Fill in the following information concerning famous rivers.

River	Location	Mouth	Length
Nile			
Amazon			
Yangtze			
Congo			
Mississippi			

© Mark Twain Media, Inc., Publishers

Torrents of Destruction

THE JOHNSTOWN FLOOD OF 1889

In 1889, Johnstown, Pennsylvania was an industrious iron and steel company town of Germans and Welsh. It had a population of 10,000, but combined with the surrounding communities, it numbered 30,000 and was growing. Located in a river valley on the Appalachian Plateau, flooding had always been a concern in Johnstown. Snows that melted too quickly or heavy rainfall flowed naturally into the valley and into the town. The Little Conemaugh and the Stony Creek Rivers, which flowed next to the town and combined to form the Conemaugh River, were frequently overflowing into the streets, and the citizens were required to evacuate their homes. As inconvenient as this was, the rivers were a vital part of the town.

For a community that relied on commerce, transportation was important. In the early days of Johnstown, shipping along the links of the waterways provided an economical and convenient way to ship and receive goods. The interlocking canals

Canals provided transportation for people and goods in many inland areas in the early 1800s.

also provided a way for passengers to travel from Johnstown to Philadelphia and Pittsburgh. Travel on these rivers was easy in the spring. In the summer, though, the rivers became so shallow that boats were unable to navigate. For this reason, in 1840 the Pennsylvania legislature voted money to construct a dam and a reservoir to supply water for navigation during the dry summers.

Fourteen miles west of Johnstown on the Little Conemaugh, the South Fork Dam was finished in 1852. It formed a three mile long lake named Lake Conemaugh. The lake was to act as a watershed to gather the water from streams in the mountains. In the summer, this reservoir could be opened to feed the rivers that were low. The lake or reservoir was 450 feet higher than Johnstown.

A few years after the dam was finished, steam railway transportation became a popular way to move goods and to travel. Over time, the waterway system was neglected. The dam was no longer used and was sold to the South Fork Fishing and Hunting Club. They used the lake for recreational purposes. The South Fork Fishing and Hunting Club was an exclusive haven for the Pittsburgh rich. Members included Andrew Carnegie and other prominent members in the Pittsburgh area. The club repaired the dam, raised the lake level and built a clubhouse and cottages for its members. These elite members enjoyed hunting, fishing, and sailing. But after their initial repair of the dam, little effort was made to maintain it. The poor condition of the dam was no secret in Johnstown. In fact, many in Johnstown joked that someday the dam might give way. But it always held, and people did not really take such jokes seriously.

The spring of 1889 was one of the wettest in the history of Johnstown. Almost 53 inches of rain had fallen in the country. The Little Conemaugh River, the Stony Creek River, and Lake Conemaugh Reservoir were full. On May 28, 1889,

DISASTER AT A GLANCE
WHAT: A dam breaks and destroys several communities
WHERE: Johnstown, Pennsylvania
WHEN: May 31, 1889
DEATHS: 2,209
COST: $17 million

a terrific storm hit the Midwest. It began in Kansas and Nebraska, and for two days it raged through Kansas, Missouri, Illinois, Michigan, Indiana, Kentucky, and Tennessee. Not only was there heavy rain, but strong winds also accompanied the storm. The rain was heavy in Johnstown on May 30 and 31. There was water in the streets. People moved their belongings to upper stories and gathered supplies needed to wait out the deluge. They were concerned, but not worried. They considered this merely an inconvenience.

While the citizens of Johnstown were not worried, the workers at the South Fork Dam were. Since mid-morning, the water had been rising, and the workers frantically worked to increase the height of the dam. They dug another spillway to relieve the pressure they had worked to avoid, but they were unsuccessful. The president of the South Fork Fishing and Hunting Club sent telegraph warnings saying the dam might give away, but most ignored his warnings. A little after 3 p.m., the dam finally gave way. A 40-foot wall of water raged toward Johnstown at 40 miles an hour. The force of the water gobbled up houses, barns, animals, and trees and devastated several communities as it ricochetted off the hills on its rampage toward Johnstown. Railroad cars were tossed around like match sticks. Brick homes were smashed. Ironically, weaker wooden structures were not immediately destroyed but just floated.

Most people heard the roar of the water as it swept into Johnstown, but it was too late to do anything about it. The 40-foot-high wave cascaded into the town at 4:07, ravaging and destroying everything. It leveled buildings and completely destroyed four square miles of downtown Johnstown. It has been estimated that the volume of water that deluged Johnstown was equal to the amount that is carried over Niagara Falls in 36 minutes.

The assault on Johnstown only lasted ten minutes, but debris of wood, trees, and other materials had piled up 30 feet high and stretched for several acres at Stone Bridge, preventing the water from receding. Many survivors were entangled in this mass of debris, and others were floating toward it. Much of the wreckage piled at the bridge was soaked with petroleum that had spilled from a freight car. Eventually, this petroleum-soaked mass was ignited by coals from stoves in the houses that were destroyed and pressed against the pile of debris. Surviving the flood, people then had to survive and rescue others from the fire.

On June 1, the rest of the world heard about the disaster at Johnstown. Almost immediately, reporters from newspapers and magazines were sent to Johnstown to report the story. Their reports were so graphic and moving that people not only from the United States, but from 18 foreign countries, sent money, clothing, lumber, and food to help in the relief effort. About $3,743,000 was collected for the Johnstown relief fund. The American Red Cross, which was organized in 1881, arrived in Johnstown on June 5, 1889, to help the survivors. This was the first major disaster relief effort for the Red Cross. Clara Barton, the founder of the Red Cross, was among the relief workers.

When the tally had ended, it was revealed that 2,209 people had died. There were 396 children under the age of 10 who died and 98 children lost both parents. There were 99 entire families who perished. There were 777 victims who were never identified, and many others were never found. Over 1,600 homes and 280 businesses were destroyed. It was estimated that $17 million in property damage was caused by the flood.

Many people blamed the disaster on the South Fork Fishing and Hunting Club. They had bought the reservoir, repaired the old dam, raised the lake level, and failed to maintain the dam the way they should have. They felt these wealthy businessmen showed little regard for the people surrounding their club. However, no successful lawsuit was ever brought against the club or its members as a result of the catastrophe.

Name _____ Date _____

Research and Thinking for the Johnstown Flood

Use resources from the library or the Internet to find the answers to the following questions.

1. Where are the Allegheny Mountains? _____

_____

2. What was the main reason the dam was built near Jamestown? _____

_____

3. Name two reasons people wanted to build canals.

    A. _____

    B. _____

4. What was the first canal built in the United States? _____

5. How were early boats along the canal propelled. _____

_____

6. What was the first *major* canal to be constructed in the United States? _____

7. Find the following dimensions of the Erie Canal:

    A. Depth: _____ B. Width: _____ C. Length: _____

8. Name two locations the Erie Canal connected. _____

_____

9. There were parades and picnics the day before the Jamestown Flood. Why? _____

_____

10. Johnstown built an incline after the flood. Explain what an incline is, why it was built, and what makes it unique.

_____

_____

_____

11. Where is the Johnstown Flood National Memorial located? _____

_____

12. Some say Johnstown was considered a perfect candidate for a major flood. Why? _____

_____

_____

The Horse Was Named Pestilence, and the Rider was Death

THE BLACK DEATH OF THE FOURTEENTH CENTURY

Look around your school room. How many students are in your class? Thirty? Thirty-five? Suppose over the course of the year, nine or 10 of your classmates caught a serious **disease** and died. Would one of the victims be your best friend? Your teacher? You? Suppose it wasn't just your classmates, but that one out of every three of your family died. What if this disease traveled throughout your town, state, and even the whole country and one-fourth to one-third of the population of all citizens died. Too fantastic? Unrealistic? It could only happen in movies? Not necessarily. This is exactly what happened in Europe between 1347 and 1350.

A terrible **plague**, called the **Black Death**, ravaged the continent. Hundreds of people died each day. The death rate was so high that the victims could not be buried properly. Many corpses remained where they fell in the streets for several days until someone could be hired to pick them up and cart them away. For the most part, the dead did not receive a funeral and were not put in a casket or buried in a grave. They were wrapped in cloth, stacked in pits, sprinkled with lime to speed decomposition, and covered with dirt. When one pit was full, another was dug, and the process was repeated. By the time the plague ended, 25 million people had died—between one-fourth and one-third of the population of Europe. The Black Death had become the greatest disaster in the history of the world.

Some disasters are sudden and devastating. A tornado or tsunami hits so quickly that one barely has time to do anything to protect himself. Other disasters happen so slowly that they are barely noticed. That is how the Black Death began. While it is not known for sure how or where the plague began, there is some evidence that it may have begun in the **Black Sea** port of **Caffa**. Some accounts say Mongolian soldiers attacked Caffa, which was protected by high walls. The **Mongol** army was infected with the plague and forced to leave, but before they did, they **catapulted** corpses of plague victims over the walls to infect their enemy. It worked. The people in Caffa got sick, and decided to leave so they would not die. They loaded up several **merchant** ships and sailed for **Messina**, a busy seaport and commercial center in northeastern Sicily. Once they arrived, the crew was so sick that only a few were left standing. The city officials, fearing they would also become sick, would not let anyone or anything come ashore. They ordered the ship to set sail for another port. What the city officials failed to notice was that a few rats on the ship scurried down the ropes that tied the ships to the dock. These rats carried plague-**infected** fleas. The plague had come to Messina.

Once in Messina, the plague spread to other cities and villages. Anyone who had any contact with the disease

> **DISASTER AT A GLANCE**
>
> **WHAT:** An infectious plague
>
> **WHERE:** Europe
>
> **WHEN:** Between 1347 and 1350
>
> **HOW:** Infected fleas were carried by rats.
>
> **DEATHS:** 25 million
>
> **AFTERMATH:** Ended the Middle Ages and began the Renaissance. More emphasis on science and the study of medicine.

© Mark Twain Media, Inc., Publishers

became infected. Once infected, people felt a pain through their body and a boil, or **bubo**, developed in their armpits or groin area. The victim became weak, developed a headache, and vomited blood for three days. The blood vessels would break and cause internal bleeding. The dried blood under the skin would become black, giving the disease the name "Black Death." After three days, the victim would die.

People had little resistance to the disease, since poor weather had destroyed their crops, and they were already weak and hungry. Village after village was stuck by the plague. Entire families died. Villages were abandoned. Peasants died in the fields or in the road. The farm animals that did not catch the disease roamed aimlessly, uncared for. Wolves stalked wandering sheep, and in some cases, even came into town looking for food.

The disease was so frightening, people began to fear and hate each other. If a son was infected, the father would not take care of him, because he knew any contact would cause his death as well. Many felt that just by breathing the same air or smelling the foul stench of the victim would be enough to infect a person. So, some people burned **incense** to conceal the odors. They covered their faces with **scented** cloths when they went outside.

Many people felt that the plague was a curse from God. They turned to priests for comfort and advice. They prayed, but the **pestilence** continued. Some felt sound would ward off the plague. Church bells and the sound of cannons echoed throughout the countryside. Some wore good luck charms. Others went to physicians for a **bloodletting**. Still others felt that if they ignored the plague and acted happy, they would be spared. They would sing and dance for hours until they were completely exhausted. However, none of these treatments worked.

One method of protection that was somewhat successful was a self-imposed **quarantine**. In an effort to save themselves, the **nobility** and **aristocrats** fled the cities and went to live in the country. They stayed in their castles or **villas** and ate simply and avoided contact with anyone who had the plague. The poor could not do this. Consequently, more wealthy people were able to survive this dreaded disease.

One of the most discouraging aspects of this disease was that it killed many people in the village and moved on to claim other victims in the next village. Then it would return and begin its conquest again. The second time it attacked a village was never as bad as the first time. But still, to survive the plague and then have to fight it again was almost too much for some people to endure.

What people did not know at this time was that the plague was an **infectious disease** called **bubonic plague** and was usually carried by **rodents**. Infected fleas on rats and other rodents left the animal **hosts** and infected humans. The flea **regurgitated** the blood from the rat into the human, infecting the human. The infection was transmitted from person to person by the bite of fleas. The disease could also be contracted by **respiratory** contact after the infection had spread to the lungs.

The plague is usually credited with ending the period generally referred to as the **Middle Ages** and beginning a new period called the **Renaissance**. The Renaissance is a period that marks the change from medieval to modern times. During the Renaissance, less emphasis was given to **superstition** and **myths**. More emphasis was placed on science and the study of medicine. This new philosophy was also carried over into the arts and other sciences.

One final note. The bubonic plague has not been eradicated. It can still be found among rats, rabbits, squirrels, and skunks. Occasionally a hunter or someone living close to the woods will contract the disease. Fortunately, the disease can now be cured if caught in time.

Name _____ Date _____

Black Death Vocabulary

How well do you understand the following terms dealing with the Black Death? Below and to the left are a number of definitions. In the blank after each definition, write the word that is described by the definition. Use the terms given below.

Definition	**Term**
1. A military machine for heaving missiles	_____
2. One who buys and sells goods for profit	_____
3. Contaminated with a disease	_____
4. A foul odor	_____
5. A member of the nomadic people of Mongolia	_____
6. A widespread epidemic	_____
7. An illness caused by an infection, physical defect, or the environment	_____
8. A pleasant smelling smoke or odor produced by burning	_____
9. Something that has an odor	_____
10. One who is harmed or becomes sick	_____
11. A busy seaport and commercial center in northeastern Sicily	_____
12. Located in the southeastern corner of Europe, it has been a trade route, tourist attraction, and fishing area.	_____
13. A boil or swelling of the lymph node	_____
14. A middle eastern port on the Black Sea	_____
15. A serious disease that is characterized by weakness, headaches, vomiting, internal bleeding, and death	_____
16. A synonym for plague, it is usually a fatal epidemic disease	_____
17. A medieval medical treatment that involves cutting a vein and letting it bleed	_____
18. Wealthy people with high birth or rank	_____
19. Hereditary rulers	_____
20. A country estate	_____
21. Mammals such as a mice, rats, squirrels, or skunks	_____
22. An animal or plant on which or in which another animal or organism lives	_____
23. To spit up or vomit	_____
24. A disease that spreads	_____
25. The medieval time before the Renaissance	_____
26. The rebirth of art and learning in Europe from 1400 to 1600	_____
27. An irrational belief	_____
28. A fictitious story	_____

aristocrats, Black Death, Black Sea, bloodletting, bubo, Caffa, catapult, disease, host, incense, infected, infectious disease, merchant, Messina, Middle Ages, Mongol, myth, nobility, pestilence, plague, regurgitate, Renaissance, rodents, scented, stench, superstition, victim, villa

© Mark Twain Media, Inc., Publishers   82

Tropical Storms

Tropical storms go by many different names. They are sometimes called **cyclones**, **hurricanes**, or **typhoons**, depending on where they occur. For example, a tropical cyclone that occurs in the western Pacific and China Sea is called a typhoon. One that begins in the equatorial regions of the Atlantic Ocean or Caribbean Sea is called a hurricane.

Tropical storms are the most ferocious storms on earth and are formed in the tropics over the oceans. These areas are very warm, and some of the water in the ocean evaporates. The warm air picks up water, and it rises. The water then condenses and forms clouds. Cooler air rushes in to take the place of the warm air, which has risen around a column of low-pressure air called the **eye**, and the wind begins to blow. The atmospheric pressure is very low in the eye of this swirling mass of wind and clouds. The more the air rushes in, the faster the winds blow. Eventually, this becomes a **tropical disturbance**. If nothing happens to break the cycle, the wind will eventually reach 74 miles an hour, and the storm becomes a **tropical storm**. The wind can increase to up to 200 miles an hour in a tropical storm.

Many hurricanes move only over the ocean and eventually die at sea. Others head toward the land, and as they move over warm water, they continue to pick up moisture, the wind increases, and the storm grows stronger. Once they arrive over land, they can cause a great deal of damage. The wind pushes the ocean toward the sea, causing flooding along the coast. This is called a **storm surge**. The wind uproots trees and damages buildings. The waves pound the shore and destroy beachfront homes and condominiums. Heavy rain causes flooding.

After the tropical storm comes on land, it begins to lose its power. The warm ocean is the fuel for the storm. It gives the storm moisture and causes the wind to increase. Once over land, the storm loses its source of fuel and begins to die.

While people living in the United States may be more familiar with the hurricanes that have occurred in the United States, there have been many very destructive typhoons in other countries. Here are a few:

The Deadliest World Cyclones

Location	Year	Deaths
1. India	1864	70,000
2. India	1942	40,000
3. Pakistan	1965	47,000
4. Pakistan	1970	200,000
5. Bangladesh	1991	131,000

Name _____ Date _____

Hurricane Vocabulary

How well do you understand the following terms dealing with hurricanes? Below and to the left are a number of definitions. In the blank after each definition, write the word that is described by the definition. Use resources from the library or Internet to find the answers. Use the terms given below.

Definition	**Term**
1. The calm center of the tropical cyclone	_____
2. A warning that winds of 74 m.p.h. or higher associated with a hurricane are expected in a specific area within 24 hours	_____
3. A rise in sea level accompanying a hurricane that is higher than it would have been without the hurricane	_____
4. A metric measurement of air pressure	_____
5. A measure of speed equal to one nautical mile per hour	_____
6. The combination of a storm surge and normal tide	_____
7. A barrier built to cushion the powerful force of the waves as they slam against the shore	_____
8. A tropical cyclone found in the north Pacific Ocean west of the International Date Line	_____
9. An atmospheric closed circulation that rotates counterclockwise in the Northern Hemisphere and clockwise in the Southern Hemisphere	_____
10. Term used for Northern Hemisphere cyclones east of the International Dateline to the Greenwich Meridian	_____
11. A hurricane with winds 131–155 m.p.h.	_____
12. A hurricane with winds 111–130 m.p.h.	_____
13. A hurricane with winds 96–110 m.p.h.	_____
14. A hurricane with winds 155 m.p.h. or more	_____
15. A hurricane with winds 74–95 m.p.h.	_____
16. A tropical cyclone with winds of less than 39 m.p.h.	_____
17. A ring of thunderstorms surrounding a storm's eye	_____
18. An announcement that a hurricane may threaten within 24 to 36 hours	_____
19. A scale that ranks storms according to their potential for damage	_____
20. The time of the year having a high incidence of hurricanes	_____

category 1, category 2, category 3, category 4, category 5, cyclone, eye, eye wall, knot, hurricane season, hurricane watch, hurricane warning, millibar, Saffir-Simpson scale, sea wall, storm surge, storm tide, tropical depression, typhoon

© Mark Twain Media, Inc., Publishers

A Killer Stalks the Resort
THE GALVESTON HURRICANE OF 1900

Galveston after the hurricane of 1900

View of a hurricane from above

Galveston, Texas, located on Galveston Island just off the coast of Texas, has a long and rich history. Galveston Island was the home to the Karankawa Indians in the 1500s. In the 1600s, Spanish explorers "discovered" the island, and in 1817, the pirate Jean Lafitte made Galveston Island his home base. By the mid nineteenth century, Galveston's harbor was an active international port. Galveston grew, and by 1900, it had a population of almost 38,000 and was connected to the mainland by a long wagon bridge and three wooden railroad trestles.

Galveston was also well-known as a resort town famous for sand beaches and spectacular sunsets. Unfortunately, the sand beaches were only about nine feet above sea level at the highest point. At some points, the streets were only four feet above sea level. This low level did not seem a problem for the businesses or the people who lived in Galveston, though. Since Galveston had experienced major storms in the past with little loss of life, most people felt that the slope of the sea bottom protected them from the large waves that are so destructive during hurricanes.

A hurricane, which would disprove that theory once and for all, began on August 27, 1900, over the Atlantic, just west of the Cape Verde Islands, about 4,000 miles from Galveston. It moved west and gained strength as it passed over Puerto Rico, the Dominican Republic, Haiti, and Cuba and headed for the Gulf of Mexico and the Gulf Coast. At this point, it was not considered a hurricane, but just a tropical storm.

On the fourth of September, when the storm was over Cuba, the Weather Bureau in Washington, D.C., issued its first warning by telegraph of a tropical storm over Cuba that was moving northward. Since a tropical storm is less severe than a hurricane, there was little cause for concern. However, by September 5, when the storm hit the Florida Keys and headed toward the coast, it had become a major hurricane.

On September 7, 1900, Galveston was experiencing a pleasant day. The temperature was in the 80s, but it was cloudy. There were people at the beach swimming, having fun, and enjoying the waves that were just beginning to grow. The size and strength of the waves continued to increase and were so fascinating that many people came to the beach to watch in wonder. By the next morning, September 8, however, the wonder had been changed to concern. The tide had

> **DISASTER AT A GLANCE**
> **WHAT:** A devastating hurricane
> **WHERE:** Galveston Island just off the coast of Texas
> **WHEN:** September 8–9, 1900
> **WHY:** Galveston was barely above sea level. There was not enough of a warning. Poor escape routes.
> **DEATHS:** About 6,000 in Galveston were killed, and another 4,000–6,000 people living on the Texas coastline were also killed.
> **AFTERMATH:** Galveston built a sea wall and raised the level of the island.

risen and was almost five feet above normal. Since all of Galveston Island was only between four and nine feet above sea level, many streets near the beach and some sections of the city were already under water.

By this time, the wagon bridge and train trestles connecting Galveston to the mainland were submerged, and the sea continued to rise. It was too late to escape to the mainland. Cottages near the beach began to wash away. Then it started to rain, and the storm became worse. The water rose to 15 feet above the streets, and the winds blew at over 120 miles per hour, reducing the entire island to rubble. The buildings that were not destroyed by the wind were pounded to pieces by the waves.

When the storm subsided and dawn came, the horror of the storm was revealed. There was a three-mile mound of rubble and dead bodies. Entire families were killed, and almost everyone had lost at least one family member. The island was littered with thousands of human bodies, as well as the carcasses of horses, cows, chickens, and dogs. It is estimated that about 6,000 in Galveston were killed by the hurricane. That is about one out of every six inhabitants. In addition, between 4,000 and 6,000 people living on the Texas coastline near Galveston were also killed.

Morgues were jammed, and undertakers were overwhelmed with bodies. The weather was hot, and the health of the survivors made it apparent that normal burial was impossible. There were just too many bodies to deal with. A burial at sea was suggested. Several hundred bodies were hauled to the ocean, weighted down, and thrown into the Gulf. However, the tide returned many of the corpses to the Galveston beaches. Burning seemed to be the best solution. However, the smoke from the funeral pyres hung over the city for days.

Galveston Learns From the Hurricane

The great hurricane showed Galvestonians that their city was not immune from the destruction of hurricanes, so they took steps to make sure they were protected in the future. Since they felt that much of the damage was done from large powerful waves that battered the island, they decided to build a sea wall to protect them from future storms. This barrier would be a breakwater to cushion the powerful force of the waves as they slammed against the island. The wall was finished on July 29, 1904, and is about 10 miles long, 17 feet high, and about five feet thick.

The citizens also decided to raise the level of the entire island to avoid future flooding. They pumped sand from the Gulf and raised the street level 17 feet above the sea wall. This meant everything in the entire city had to be raised—every building that remained standing, all fire hydrants, rail tracks, water pipes, and even the trees and shrubs—in short, everything on the island was raised. This project was finished in 1910.

Their strategy seems to have worked. The city has been hit by several other powerful hurricanes since the sea wall was built and the island raised, but the damage has not been anywhere near that of the 1900 hurricane. An enormous hurricane in 1961, Hurricane Carla, pounded Galveston with sea surges up to 19 feet and 170 m.p.h. winds, but only 45 people died. Just as important as building the sea wall and raising the city is the fact that we are now able to predict and warn people approximately when and where a hurricane will occur. The tragedy of Galveston occurred because there was no early warning and no evacuation.

The Galveston Hurricane of 1900 remains the greatest natural disaster in the history of the United States. But it is not the most severe hurricane ever to hit the United States. There have been many others of about the same intensity and two that were stronger—a hurricane that struck the Florida Keys in 1935 and Hurricane Camille, which hit the Gulf Coast in 1969. But the Galveston Hurricane caused more deaths than any other.

Camille Was No Lady

HURRICANE CAMILLE OF 1969

The Galveston Hurricane of 1900 killed more people, and the 1935 hurricane that struck the Florida Keys was more powerful than Camille. In fact, there have been at least four other hurricanes that were more costly than Camille. But no storm had ever caused such widespread destruction and terror as Camille did on August 17, 1969.

Camille was a small but very intense storm that was formed off the coast of Africa and became a hurricane just south of Cuba on August 15, 1969. It began quickly growing that night as it moved into the Gulf of Mexico. By noon on the 17th, 210 mile per hour winds struck Louisiana and then raged along the Mississippi coast pounding Venice, Waveland, Bay St. Louis, Pass Christian, Long Beach, Gulfport, Biloxi, and Ocean Springs, through Alabama, up to West Virginia and Virginia, and finally back out to sea.

Camille, the United States' second strongest twentieth century hurricane, created a tremendous tide that caused the Mississippi River to rise. At Buras, Louisiana, the river breached the 15-foot levee and flooded the town in over 12 feet of water. Waveland, Mississippi, was almost completely destroyed. Another resort community, Pass Christian, did not fare any better. It was also leveled. What the wind did not destroy in Pass Christian, a tidal wave about 20 feet high, which covered the town, did. A six-story bank building was destroyed, and all that remained in its place was the vault.

The storm continued northeast into Pascagoula, Mississippi. The residents of this community not only had to endure the high winds and rain, they had an additional challenge—snakes! The storm forced hundreds of deadly water moccasin snakes out of the marshes into the town in search of food and shelter. The terrified citizens had to organize to rid their city of the snakes before they could go about the business of assessing the damage and rebuilding their homes and businesses.

While most of the damage was done on the Gulf Coast and in Alabama, Camille was by no means finished. She continued her path of destruction to West Virginia and Virginia with strong winds and heavy rains. The rains, which dumped as much as 10 inches in just a few hours, caused flooding and mudslides. People drowned, roads were swamped, and homes were ruined.

When the fury of Camille had ended, about 250 people had died and another 100 were missing. The damage is estimated at over 6.4 billion in 1998 dollars. Five thousand homes were completely destroyed, while 40,000 were heavily damaged.

Although Camille caused a great deal of death and destruction, it could have been worse. Had the full fury of the storm struck New Orleans, just a few miles from where Camille came ashore, it could have had even more tragic consequences. New Orleans is the city in the United States most vulnerable to storm surge damage, because parts of New Orleans lie below sea level. What makes it even worse is that New Orleans is surrounded by water. The Mississippi is to the south, Lake Pontchartrain is to the north, and Lake Borgne is to the east. In addition, there are smaller lakes, marshes, and bayous surrounding the city. There is a system of levees designed to protect New Orleans, but a direct assault the magnitude of Camille, could cause a storm surge great enough to rupture the levees that protect the city. If this were to happen, roads and highways could be swamped, making it difficult for residents flee.

DISASTER AT A GLANCE

WHAT: The second most intense U.S. hurricane

WHERE: Initially it hit Louisiana, then raged along the Mississippi coast, through Alabama, up to West Virginia and Virginia, and finally back out to sea.

WHEN: August 17, 1969

COST: 6.4 billion in 1998 dollars

DEATHS: 250 people died and another 100 were missing.

AFTERMATH: Citizens in the path of hurricanes took warnings more seriously.

Andrew Was No Gentleman
Hurricane Andrew of 1992

There is a saying among the people who live along the southern coastline of the United States. "The most beautiful day you have seen is the one that comes just before a hurricane." That was certainly the case on August 23, 1992, in Homestead, Florida. The bright, beautiful skies were punctuated with high cirrus clouds. Rising swells from the nearby ocean provided a soothing rhythm, which an observer would have found relaxing if he had not heard of the approaching hurricane that was now battering the Bahamas with 150 m.p.h. winds.

It had been 27 years since South Florida had experienced a severe hurricane. A large number of the residents—many retirees—did not know how destructive hurricanes could be. They were unaware that in 1935 the most intense storm to strike the United States in the twentieth century came ashore in the Florida Keys. While this storm only killed 408 people in the sparsely populated area, the wind was so strong that it literally ripped away the clothes and tore the skin off those who did not seek shelter. Then in 1969, the second most powerful hurricane to strike the United States, Hurricane Camille, struck Mississippi, then traveled north causing flash floods that killed 154 in Virginia's mountains. All told, Camille killed 250 people and another 100 were reported missing.

The third most intense hurricane to hit the United States—Andrew—arrived on August 24, 1992. Hurricane Andrew slammed into South Florida, bulldozing everything in its path. It came ashore just 23 miles south of downtown Miami, sparing the city the full impact of the storm. The 140 m.p.h. winds with gusts up to 266 m.p.h. and a storm surge of over 16 feet, were not so kind to other areas. The storm flattened Homestead, Florida, and devastated parts of Miami. Homestead, a town of 32,000, just 20 miles south of Miami, looked as though a 10-mile-wide tornado had passed through the town, destroying everything in its path.

Andrew killed 15 people in Dade County, and it was estimated 25 others died as an indirect result of the storm. The storm caused terrific damage to homes. Up to one-quarter of a million people were left homeless. Andrew also had a severe impact on the environment and ecosystem in Date County. Ninety-percent of South Dade mangroves, native pinelands, and tropical hardwood hammocks, along with 33 percent of the coral reefs at Biscayne National Park, were damaged. It also left a mountain of debris that took years to clean up.

Andrew hit Florida fast and hard and moved quickly over Florida, then out into the Gulf. Over 1.5 million residents of Louisiana evacuated as the storm approached. Fortunately, the hurricane struck a sparsely populated section of south-central Louisiana, but still took another eight lives. It moved slowly across Louisiana toward Mississippi, leveling homes as it advanced. Its path was marked by drenching rains and tornadoes.

By the time Andrew had finished its destructive march, it was ranked not only the third most intense storm to hit the United States, but also the costliest disaster in U.S. history. It caused 28.5 billion dollars in damage. Homestead suffered the most:

- 108,000 homes were demolished.
- 250,000 residents were displaced.
- 8,000 businesses were destroyed
- Thousands of residents left and never returned.
- The local economy lost 11,000 jobs and $406 million a year.
- Homestead Air Force Base was destroyed and not rebuilt as an active base, but turned it into a reserve base. It now is one-third its former size and has one-tenth the military personnel, civilians, and dependents who were part of the base.

DISASTER AT A GLANCE
WHAT: Costliest U.S. hurricane
WHERE: Homestead, Florida
WHEN: August 24, 1992
COST: 32.3 billion in 1998 dollars
DEATHS: 52 directly and indirectly
AFTERMATH: Thousands of residents left Homestead and never returned. Jobs and industry were lost.

Name _____ Date _____

Three Infamous U.S. Hurricanes

There have been many well-known hurricanes, but three seem to stand out from the rest. They are the Galveston Hurricane of 1900, Camille, and Andrew. How much do you know about each? Listed below are statements that relate to one of the three hurricanes. Before each statement are the letters "G," which represents Galveston, "C," which represents Camille, and "A," which represents Andrew. Circle the letter to which the statement pertains.

G C A   1. It destroyed Homestead, Florida.
G C A   2. The storm created a tide that caused the Mississippi River to rise.
G C A   3. This storm struck the island that was the former home of Jean Lafitte, the pirate.
G C A   4. It occurred on August 24, 1992.
G C A   5. It came ashore just 23 miles south of downtown Miami.
G C A   6. This storm came ashore in Texas.
G C A   7. The third most intense hurricane to hit the U.S.
G C A   8. As a result of this storm, 250 people died and 100 were missing.
G C A   9. It displaced 250,000 residents.
G C A 10. It occurred on August 17, 1969.
G C A 11. As a result of this storm, the town tried to bury the dead at sea.
G C A 12. No storm had ever caused such widespread destruction and terror.
G C A 13. The local economy lost 11,000 jobs and $406 million.
G C A 14. The victims of this storm were burned instead of buried.
G C A 15. Fifty-two people died either directly or indirectly as a result of this storm.
G C A 16. This was the second most intense U.S. hurricane.
G C A 17. It demolished 108,000 homes.
G C A 18. It was the greatest natural disaster in the history of the United States.
G C A 19. It occurred on September 8–9, 1900.
G C A 20. It came ashore in Louisiana, then raged along the Mississippi coast.
G C A 21. This storm was so destructive because of no early warning system and no evacuation.
G C A 22. It caused 28.5 billion dollars in damage.
G C A 23. It caused damage amounting to 6.4 billion in 1998 dollars.
G C A 24. All told, this storm killed almost 12,000 people.
G C A 25. The island this storm hit was between four and nine feet above sea level.
G C A 26. The storm destroyed 5,000 homes and damaged 40,000.
G C A 27. This hurricane caused more deaths than any other.
G C A 28. The storm struck just a few miles from New Orleans.
G C A 29. It destroyed 8,000 businesses.
G C A 30. This storm forced hundreds of deadly snakes into the town.
G C A 31. As a result of this storm, the city it hit built a flood wall.
G C A 32. This storm caused heavy rains and mudslides in Virginia and West Virginia.
G C A 33. As a result of this storm, the city it hit raised their entire city.
G C A 34. It was the costliest hurricane to hit the United States.
G C A 35. This hurricane damaged many species in the Florida ecosystem.

© Mark Twain Media, Inc., Publishers

The Worst U.S. Hurricanes of the Twentieth Century

What was the worst hurricane disaster in recent United States history? It depends on how you define *worst*. The word *worst* can mean the deadliest, that is the hurricane that killed the most people. It can also mean the hurricane that caused the most damage. Or it can even mean the hurricane that was the most intense or strongest, even if it did not kill anyone or cause much damage. Listed below are the U.S. hurricanes that can be considered the "worst" in each of these three categories.

The Deadliest U.S. Hurricanes

Hurricane	Year	Category	Deaths
1. Galveston , TX	1900	4	8000–12,000
2. Florida	1928	4	1,836
3. Florida Keys & TX	1919	4	600
4. New England	1938	3	600
5. Florida Keys	1935	5	408

The exact number of people killed in the Galveston Hurricane is not known. It is estimated that about 6,000 where killed in Galveston and another 4,000–6000 were killed along the Texas coast.

The Costliest U.S. Hurricanes

Hurricane	Year	Category	Damage
1. Andrew	1992	4	$32,300,000,000
2. Hugo	1989	4	9,000,000,000
3. Agnes	1972	1	7,950,000,000
4. Betsy	1965	3	7,870,870,000
5. Camille—LA/MS	1969	5	6,430,500,800

These amounts are inflation adjusted to 1998 dollars.

The Most Intense U.S. Hurricanes

Hurricane	Year	Category	Millibars (Inches)
1. Florida Keys	1935	5	892 (26.35)
2. Camille	1969	5	909 (26.84)
3. Andrew	1992	4	922 (27.23)
4. Florida Keys & TX	1919	4	927 (27.37)
5. Lake Okeechobee, FL	1928	4	929 (27.43)

Hurricane Gilbert, which struck south of Brownsville, was a category 5 and had the lowest pressure recorded in the northern hemisphere (888 mbs). Gilbert inflicted a great deal of damage on Jamacia and Mexico, but by the time it arrived in the United States, it was considered only a weakening tropical depression.

Name _____ Date _____

Research and Thinking for Hurricanes

1. In the category *Costliest U.S. Hurricanes*, the sentence, "These figures are inflation adjusted to 1998 dollars" is used. In your own words, explain what that sentence means. Give an example.

_____

_____

_____

2. The hurricane in Galveston in 1900 claimed the lives of over 10,000 people. Yet it was less powerful than the hurricane in 1935 in the Florida Keys and Hurricane Camille in 1969. Why did the hurricane in Galveston kill more people?

_____

_____

_____

3. Hurricane Agnes which struck in 1972, was only a category 1 hurricane, and yet it caused more damage than Camille, which was a stronger category 5 hurricane. Why?

_____

_____

_____

4. Some of the hurricanes on the list have names, but others do not. Why?

_____

_____

5. How are the names selected?

_____

_____

6. What exactly causes the damage during a hurricane?

_____

_____

7. Why are hurricanes sometimes considered more of a threat today, in spite of the fact that there is more of a warning system in place?

_____

_____

_____

The Day the Earth Shook and the Dinosaurs Died
THE YUCATAN PENINSULA ASTEROID OF 65 MILLION YEARS AGO

Every so often, the newspapers will report that an **astronomer** has discovered an **asteroid** speeding toward the earth. With high tech computers, the astronomer is able to estimate the size of the asteroid and approximately when it will be close to earth. Such a prediction occurred in March 1998. Scientists said that a huge asteroid called 1997 XF11 would come very close to earth at 12:30 p.m. on October 26, 2028. And it was possible, they added, that it could even collide with the earth. If it did, it would be traveling at more than 17,000 m.p.h. and would release the energy equal to two million **Hiroshima**-sized atomic bombs. Depending on where the asteroid hit, such an impact would have catastrophic consequences. It could wipe out the inhabitants of an entire region. If it landed in the ocean, it would create a tidal wave called a **tsunami** several hundred feet high, which could literally wash away all of the cities along a coast line. The life that existed after the impact would also be dismal.

Fortunately, shortly after this announcement, the scientists recalculated and announced that the asteroid would *not* come close enough to the earth for us to be concerned about. Even if they hadn't found their mistake, we would have had over three decades to prepare, and may have been able to figure out a way to avert the disaster. Even though being hit by a asteroid is a remote possibility, it has happened in the past and will probably happen again in the future. While most **comets** or asteroids miss the earth, about every century a large comet passes between the earth and the moon. It is estimated that some time within the next million years a large asteroid will strike the earth. It will cause huge fires, and the resulting dust and smoke will block out the sun so that plants will not grow and humans and animals will starve.

In fact, many scientists believe that an asteroid colliding with the earth is what destroyed the **dinosaurs**. They estimate that an asteroid 6–10 miles across collided with Earth about 65 million years ago and caused the extinction of the dinosaurs, as well as 75 percent of all other species. How did scientists develop this theory? By studying **fossils** and the earth, they learned that although dinosaurs had lived and thrived for millions of years, they became **extinct**. They discovered this by finding fossils of dinosaurs in layer after layer of **Cretaceous** rock. Then, all of a sudden, there were no fossils in succeeding layers. They also learned these facts about the death of the dinosaurs:

- It happened 65 million years ago.
- It happened fairly quickly.
- It happened in all parts of the world.
- There were about 100 different groups of dinosaurs living just before they became extinct.
- Many other land animals and plants also became extinct at about the same time.
- The animals that survived—some mammals, birds, and reptiles—were greatly reduced in numbers.

What kind of catastrophe could have caused the dinosaurs, and other plant and animal life to disappear so suddenly? Many explanations have been offered.

Asteroid collision theory. The theory many accept is that a 6- to 10-mile-wide asteroid collided with the earth. When this occurred, debris was sent into the atmosphere and probably caused a period of global darkness lasting several months. Without sunlight, many of the plants and animals that survived the impact died. Scientists arrived at this theory by studying three pieces of evidence. The first piece of evidence

> **DISASTER AT A GLANCE**
> **WHAT:** An asteroid strikes the earth
> **WHERE:** Yucatan Peninsula
> **WHEN:** 65 Million years ago
> **AFTERMATH:** All of the dinosaurs and 75 percent of all other creatures died.

for this asteroid impact explanation involves a study of **microscopic** particles of **quartz** found in 65-million-year-old sediment at different sites around the world. The deposits at all of the sites showed signs of structural cracks, which are consistent with sudden impacts such as those made by an asteroid striking the earth. Second, the scientists also found unusual concentrations of the element **iridium**. While iridium is rare on Earth, it is abundant in meteorites and asteroids. Third, there is evidence that a gigantic asteroid struck the Yucatan Peninsula 65 million years ago, about the same time the dinosaurs became extinct.

Changes in **diet** have also been considered as a possible reason dinosaurs became extinct. Dinosaurs were **herbivores**, that is they ate plants. Most of the plants on earth were nonflowering plants, such as ferns and pine trees. Dinosaurs loved this diet and ate as much as a ton of **foliage** a day. During the Cretaceous period, however, a new class of plants evolved there called **angiosperms**, which are flowering plants. This class of plants included shrubs, **deciduous** trees, leafy plants, bamboo, palms, and some flowers. Were the dinosaurs able to develop a taste for these new plants? Or did they find them indigestible? Some even believe that over a period of time angiosperms caused a slow poisoning of the dinosaurs.

A related theory deals with the **climate**. Ocean currents and wind patterns were changing. The inland seas, where many of the dinosaurs lived, were drying up. The climate was cooler and drier. The **swamps** filled with ferns were turning into **meadows** with deciduous trees and grasses. However, many believe these changes were probably too gradual to explain the sudden disappearance of the dinosaurs. And certainly it would not explain why they also died in the tropics.

Another theory deals with **volcanic activity**. Since there were many active volcanoes at this time, there must have been a great deal of **carbon monoxide** in the atmosphere, which would have trapped the **radiant heat** from the sun, causing a **greenhouse effect**. The temperature of the earth would have risen, killing off plants and animals and disrupting the delicate **ecosystem**, causing widespread **starvation** of many species. The rising temperature could have made the dinosaurs **infertile**. The volcanic activity would have also created enough **chlorine** gas to destroy the **ozone** layer. Without the ozone layer, the **ultraviolet radiation** would burn bare-skinned animals such as dinosaurs, while sparing some feathered and marine creatures.

Two other theories have also been suggested to explain the death of the dinosaurs. One is that dinosaurs were just too dumb to survive. They were outsmarted and outmaneuvered by smarter more aggressive mammals. However, a study of the brain cavities of these creatures reveals they were no less intelligent than some species that did survive. The other theory involves the eggs of the dinosaurs. Perhaps other creatures found dinosaur eggs tasty and devoured them before they could hatch. Or, maybe something in the environment caused the dinosaur eggs not to hatch.

While we may never know for sure if an asteroid killed these fascinating creatures, we do know that an asteroid struck Earth 65 million years ago, at about the same time dinosaurs became extinct. It hit the **Yucatan Peninsula** from the southeast at a 20- to 30-degree angle, and the impact was so great it send waves of **vaporized** fireballs of rock skimming the earth and strafing North America. This two-mile-deep layer of vaporized rock and other material bounced all across North America and eventually around the globe. It was like a huge **nuclear explosion** seared North America and then the rest of the world.

Investigations at the Yucatan crater seem to support this theory. Scientists have studied the huge crater and the angle at which the asteroid must have hit. Using modern technology, they have been able to determine the devastating consequences of such an occurrence. Many scientists believe this was the day the earth shook and the dinosaurs died.

© Mark Twain Media, Inc., Publishers

Name_____ Date _____

Death of the Dinosaurs Vocabulary

How well do you understand the following terms that were used in *"The Day the Earth Shook and the Dinosaurs Died"*? Below and to the left are a number of definitions. In the blank after each definition, write the word that is described by the definition. Use the terms given below.

Definition	**Term**
1. Any of the thousands of small planetoids that revolve around the sun.	_____
2. A very hard mineral composed of silica	_____
3. Deprived of food	_____
4. A large ocean wave, often caused by a seaquake	_____
5. An animal that feeds on plants	_____
6. A scientist who studies space and celestial bodies	_____
7. Converted into mist	_____
8. A plant or tree that loses its foliage at the end of the growing season	_____
9. A hard and brittle metallic element occurring in platinum ores	_____
10. A flowering plant	_____
11. The weather that is prevalent in a particular region	_____
12. The community of living organisms in a particular environment	_____
13. A gigantic reptile that existed during the Mesozoic era	_____
14. A group of leaves	_____
15. No longer alive	_____
16. A geologic period known for the development of flowering plants and the disappearance of dinosaurs	_____
17. A theory that holds that an asteroid collided with the earth and destroyed the dinosaurs	_____
18. Energy emissions in the form of rays or waves	_____
19. Not capable of producing offspring	_____
20. A Japanese city that was destroyed by the first atomic bomb dropped during World War II	_____
21 A colorless, odorless, poisonous gas	_____
22. A celestial body with a head of solid nucleus surrounded by a nebulous curved vapor tail	_____
23. So small it can only be seen with a microscope	_____
24. Eating and drinking according to a system	_____

© Mark Twain Media, Inc., Publishers

Name_____ Date _____

25. The range of invisible radiation wavelengths just beyond the violet _____

    in the visible spectrum

26. A greenish-yellow gas that is used to destroy germs in water   _____

27. An imprint of an organism from the past   _____

28. A term that explains how the atmosphere helps warm the earth's   _____

    air

angiosperm	asteroid	asteroid collision theory	astronomer
carbon monoxide	climate	chlorine	comet	Cretaceous
deciduous	diet	dinosaur	ecosystem	extinct
foliage	fossil	greenhouse effect	herbivore
Hiroshima	infertile	iridium	microscopic	quartz
radiation	starve	tsunami	ultraviolet	vaporized

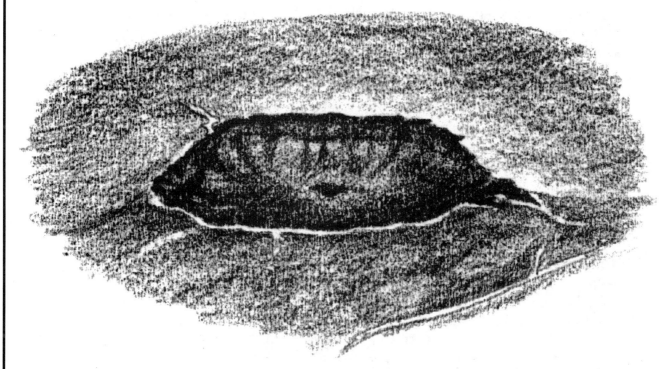

Crater caused by the impact of a meteorite

© Mark Twain Media, Inc., Publishers

Name _____ Date _____

Extinction of the Dinosaurs Report

Divide students into several groups. Each group will be assigned one theory explaining how dinosaurs became extinct. There does not have to be a group for each theory, but there should be more than three different groups. Some of the theories to be considered are that the dinosaurs were destroyed by:

- an asteroid or a comet;
- volcanic eruption or eruptions;
- change in the plant life during the Cretaceous period, altering the diet of the dinosaurs;
- change in climate;
- the development of smarter, faster mammals that destroyed them or ate their eggs;
- other theories the students might develop.

Follow these steps to complete the assignment.

1. As a group the students will gather information and develop arguments to support the group's theory.
2. Each group will write a report explaining its theory and providing reasons why the group believes it is the most logical explanation for the disappearance of the dinosaurs. The report will include the following information.
   - An introduction, stating the question they are trying to answer and various theories that have been presented to answer the question.
   - An explanation of the theory the group supports.
   - A background and the history of the theory's development, if possible.
   - Arguments to support the group's theory.
   - Arguments that criticize other theories.
   - Any other relative information.
   - A conclusion.
3. After the reports are finished, each group will have an opportunity to orally present its paper to the class.
4. Each member of the group will be expected to participate in the presentation. Perhaps each person will present one portion of the paper.
5. After the presentation, the class will question the group's findings and debate the theory.
6. The process will be repeated for each group.
7. The papers may then be combined on the computer and printed as a book entitled, *The Death of the Dinosaurs: A Study of the Theories Surrounding Their Extinction*. The class can decide if their book should stress one theory over another.
8. Copies of the book should be kept in the classroom for future classes and presented to the school library.

© Mark Twain Media, Inc., Publishers

Name _____   Date _____

Making a Fossil

Fossils are what remains of organisms that have been preserved by burial under layers of sedimentary material. Scientists have been able to learn a lot about the earth and how life evolved by studying fossils. Most of us have seen fossils, but did you know you can make your own? Here is how you do it.

What You Will Need:

- Two paper cups
- A piece of modeling clay large enough to fill $\frac{1}{4}$ of a paper cup
- Enough plaster of Paris to fill $\frac{1}{2}$ the paper cup
- $\frac{1}{4}$ cup of water
- A seashell

Follow these steps:

1. Roll the clay into a ball and flatten it on a table until it is about 1 inch thick.
2. Trim the clay with a dull knife so that it will fit into the bottom of one of the cups.
3. With the flat side up, push the clay into the bottom of one of the cups.
4. Gently press the shell into the clay until it is buried halfway.
5. Carefully remove the shell. You can see what your fossil is going to look like.
6. Into another cup mix $\frac{1}{2}$ cup of plaster of Paris and $\frac{1}{4}$ cup of water.
7. Let sit for five minutes.
8. When the plaster of Paris has thickened (after about five minutes) pour it into the other cup, on top of the clay with the impression of the shell.
9. After about an hour, when the plaster of Paris is hard, tear the sides of the paper cup and remove the clay from the plaster. Be careful, the plaster may not be completely hardened.
10. Pull the clay away. The fossil is in the plaster of Paris.
11. Carefully smooth any rough edges on the plaster.
12. Let it dry for one or two days, and your fossil is complete. The fossil must dry slowly, so do not put it in the oven, microwave, or sun or use a hair dryer to hurry the job. If you do, it might crack.

Death on the Mississippi
THE *SULTANA* STEAMSHIP EXPLOSION OF 1865

When the Civil War ended on April 15, 1865, the country breathed a sigh of relief. The war between the states had taken a terrible toll. Over 600,000 soldiers had been killed. Estates, farms, businesses, and fortunes had been lost. Entire cities had been destroyed over the four years the war had raged. Perhaps no one was happier the Civil War ended than the 5,000 Union soldiers in Camp Fisk outside Vicksburg, Mississippi. These soldiers had previously been imprisoned in Andersonville and Cahaba prison camps. Civil War prisons were terrible. Poor sanitary conditions and lack of food and warm clothing made life in a Civil War prison unbearable. It has been reported that the death rate in prison camps was 10 times greater than the death rate on the battlefield. Prisoners that managed to survive prison camps were usually sick and malnourished. It was common for prisoners to lose half of their weight while in prison.

So, when word came of the armistice, the prisoners of Camp Fisk were joyous. They were sick and weak, but they talked of their release and of their homecoming. They wanted to get home as soon as possible and return to their jobs and families. Since much of the nation's railroad system had been destroyed by the war, the federal government made arrangements for the soldiers to be returned to their homes on steamboats.

Steamboats were a fast and relatively cheap form of moving people and goods along the Ohio, Mississippi, and other rivers and streams of the Mississippi Valley. Steamboats made the New Orleans seaport almost as important as New York. Even though steamboats were a popular form of travel, they were dangerous. Fires and running aground were a constant threat. But the danger most feared by river men was a boiler explosion. It could kill more people and cause more damage than any other kind of accident. Unfortunately, boiler explosions were common, averaging a couple a week.

What made the boiler explosions even more dangerous was the materials from which steamboats were made. They were made of wood, so they could be light, fast, and cheap. Highly flammable varnishes made the decks and wood attractive, but they also made the boats tinder boxes ready to be ignited. What made matters even worse was that, during the war, both sides eliminated the few safety regulations that had

---

DISASTER AT A GLANCE

WHAT: Boiler explosion on the *Sultana,* a steamboat

WHERE: On the Mississippi River seven miles north of Memphis, Tennessee

WHEN: After midnight on April 27, 1865

WHY: A defective boiler is patched rather than replaced. The boat is overloaded.

DEATHS: About 1,700

© Mark Twain Media, Inc., Publishers   98

been in place in an effort to speed the shipments of troops, weapons, food, and equipment. Safety was ignored, and many fatal accidents were the result.

These dangers did not worry the prisoners of Fisk prison. Neither were they worried about the mighty Mississippi, which was in flood stage. Snow melt in the north and spring rains, coupled with levees and dams that had been neglected during the war, made the river a dangerous place to be. Nevertheless, the soldiers were eager to get home, and the steamboat was the quickest way to get there.

The swollen river also did not worry J. Cass Mason, owner and captain of the *Sultana*, a sidewheeler. The *Sultana*, one of the fastest and most reliable boats on the river, was 260 feet long and hauled passengers and goods from New Orleans, making stops in Vicksburg, Memphis, Cairo, Evansville, Louisville, and Cincinnati. When the *Sultana* arrived in Vicksburg on April 24 to take on passengers, cargo, and soldiers, it was learned that one of the boilers had ruptured. Instead of replacing the boiler, which would have been costly and taken time, the chief engineer of the *Sultana* had a Vicksburg boiler maker apply a temporary patch. Business was slack, and steamboats had to compete for the little business there was. The opportunity to transport soldiers was so important it could not be postponed.

Captain Mason, knew he would be paid $5 for each soldier and $10 for each officer he transported, so he wanted to get as many soldiers as possible assigned to the *Sultana*. In spite of the fact the passenger capacity for the *Sultana* was only 376, Mason negotiated a deal that allowed him to transport about 2,000 soldiers aboard the *Sultana*. He was able to do this because he exaggerated the capacity of the *Sultana*, and he paid a "commission" to Colonel Ruben B. Hatch, Chief Quarter Master of the Department of the Mississippi in charge of arranging transportation for the Union Soldiers, to put as many soldiers on the *Sultana* as would fit.

In addition to the soldiers, there were 100 civilians, 100 hogsheads of sugar and wine, and 100 head of assorted livestock. The decks were literally sagging from all of the weight and needed to be propped up so they did not collapse. The passengers were warned to stay distributed on both sides of the ship. If everyone went to the port side, for example, as they were leaving the shore, the ship might tip over.

In spite of the patched boiler, the swift current, and the extreme weight of the passengers and cargo, the *Sultana* inched its way northward. The night was cool, and the men tried to crowd near the boiler in order to keep warm. A little after 2:00 a.m. on April 27, 1865, just seven miles north of Memphis, Tennessee, the *Sultana's* boiler exploded. The explosion was so loud and the flash was so bright that it was heard and seen in Memphis. The boat was nearly blown in two and began to sink. Scorching water and red hot coals rained down on those on the deck. Many passengers were killed instantly. Others were burned and scalded and died from the fire. Still others were thrown into the dark, raging river and drowned. The passengers who were not killed needed to choose between flaming death on the boat or drowning in the river. Many chose to jump into the river, even though some of them could not swim. These passengers not only had to fight the furious Mississippi, they had to fight each other to survive. They fought and clawed for planks, logs, and debris to grasp so they would not drown. The water was like ice, and since most of the soldiers were sick and malnourished, they eventually died.

The exact number of people killed in this tragedy is unknown, since the records of the soldiers boarding the ship were not complete. Most believe that somewhere between 1,500 and 1,900 died as a result of the disaster. The *Sultana* tragedy is the United States's worst maritime disaster and is one of the most terrible steamship disasters in all of history. Oddly, this disaster received only a small amount of attention at the time. There were few newspaper accounts of the tragedy, and even today, it is not found in many history or reference books.

Name_____ Date _____

Reading a Map

The story about the *Sultana* tragedy mentioned several locations: Andersonville Prison; Cairo, Illinois; Cincinnati, Ohio; Cahaba Prison; Evansville, Indiana; Helena, Arkansas; Louisville, Kentucky; Memphis, Tennessee; New Orleans, Louisiana; St. Louis, Missouri; and Vicksburg, Mississippi. Using an atlas, find these locations on the map above and write the name of the location opposite the appropriate number below.

1._____   2._____   3._____

4._____   5._____   6._____

7._____   8._____   9._____

10._____   11._____

Sultana Study Question

The article says that, "Oddly, this disaster received only a small amount of attention at the time. There were few newspaper accounts of the tragedy, and even today, it is not found in many history or reference books." Why do you suppose this is?

_____

_____

_____

_____

_____

© Mark Twain Media, Inc., Publishers   100

Name _____ Date _____

Steamboats and the Mississippi Quiz

After researching steamboats in the library or on the Internet, see how much you have learned by circling the correct answers to the questions below.

1. What is the *main* reason steamboats were a popular method of transportation?

    A. They had gambling.

    B. They provided entertainment.

    C. They were relatively cheap.

    D. They were safe.

2. Who invented the first successful steam *engine*?

    A. Fitch

    B. Shreve

    C. Watt

    D. Morse

3. Which of the following was not involved in the development of the steamboat?

    A. Fitch

    B. Shreve

    C. Fulton

    D. Morse

4. What was the first steamship to cross the Atlantic?

    A. The *Titanic*

    B. The *Savannah*

    C. The *Sultana*

    D. The *General Slocum*

5. Which of the following was a famous steamboat captain?

    A. Steamboat Willy

    B. Captain Courageous

    C. Mark Twain

    D. Captain Kirk

6. What was this captain's real name?

    A. Mark Trail

    B. Samuel Gompers

    C. William Shatner

    D. Samuel Clemens

7. What was this captain's hometown?

    A. Cairo, Illinois

    B. Vicksburg, Mississippi

    C. Memphis, Tennessee

    D. Hannibal, Missouri

8. What was the approximate number of steamboats in use in 1860?

    A. 20

    B. 200

    C. 2,000

    D. 20,000

9. What was the name of the first successful steamboat?

    A. The *Sultana*

    B. The *Vicksburg*

    C. The *Clermont*

    D. The *Deep Blue Sea*

10. Who developed the first *successful* steamboat?

    A. Robert Fulton

    B. Steamboat Bill

    C. Robert Louis Stevenson

    D. Fulton Sheen

© Mark Twain Media, Inc., Publishers

Name _____ Date _____

11. What does "Mark Twain" mean?

    A. The water is 12 feet deep   C. Look out for snags

    B. Railroad bridge ahead   D. Logs in the river

12. What is a nickname for the Mississippi?

    A. Old Man River   C. Mighty Mississippi

    B. Father of Waters   D. All of the above

13. Which state is not located along the Mississippi?

    A. Louisiana   C. Arkansas

    B. Mississippi   D. Georgia

14. In 1861, many steamboats stopped operating. Why?

    A. The development of the Transcontinental Railroad

    B. The beginning of the War Between the States

    C. Danger of fire and boiler explosions

    D. None of the above

15. What did the steamboat bring to our nation?

    A. Businesses   C. Jobs

    B. New Towns   D. All of the above

16. Which river empties into the Mississippi?

    A. Missouri   C. Arkansas

    B. Ohio   D. All of the above

17. What was the danger most feared by river men?

    A. Indians   C. Snags

    B. Explosions   D. Gamblers

18. John Fitch demonstrated his steamboat on which river in 1787?

    A. Delaware River   C. Hudson River

    B. Potomac River   D. James River

19. Who was Robert Fulton's partner in his steamboat venture?

    A. Mark Twain   C. Robert Livingston

    B. John Fitch   D. James Rumsey

20. Which steamboat made the first trip down the Ohio and Mississippi Rivers?

    A. The *Clermont*   C. The *Savannah*

    B. The *New Orleans*   D. The *Delta Queen*

© Mark Twain Media, Inc., Publishers

The Unthinkable Strikes the Unsinkable

THE *TITANIC* TRAGEDY OF 1912

In 1907, Lord Pirrie and J. Bruce Ismay developed plans for the SS *Titanic*—the largest, fastest, most luxurious ship ever built. On March 31, 1909, the Harland and Wolff shipyard began construction on the mighty ship for the White Star Line. When the 50,000 horsepower ship was finally completed in 1912, it cost $7,500,000.

The finished ship had nine decks and was as tall as an 11-story building. It was 900 feet long—as long as four city blocks—and weighed 46,328 tons. Although the *Titanic* was enormous, its main objective was, ultimately, the comfort of its guests. All of the passengers experienced a luxury they had never before known aboard a ship.

Still, there was no questioning the division of the classes, and each passenger got exactly what he or she paid for, with prices ranging from $30 (comparable to $345 in today's money) for the cheapest third-class ticket, all the way up to $4,350 (comparable to $40,000 in today's money) for the most expensive first-class ticket.

For the first-class passengers, the *Titanic* offered a gymnasium, swimming pool, Turkish baths, barber shops, and exceptional dining facilities, including a Parisian sidewalk cafe complete with French waiters and strolling musicians. Although second class could not compare to first class, they still had larger, more luxurious accommodations than on any other ship. The *Titanic* even had an elevator for the second class, something no ship had ever before had. Even the third class was not forgotten. Their accommodations included better quality dining and a public gathering place. In order to attend to each and every need of the approximately 1,300 passengers on board, the ship employed a crew of nearly 900.

In addition to its unsurpassed luxury, the *Titanic* was advertised as being the first unsinkable ship. Even if it was not absolutely unsinkable, it was surely the safest ship ever built. To ensure this safety, it had 16 watertight compartments that were separated by emergency doors that could be dropped in a matter of seconds by simply flipping an electrical switch from the bridge. This meant that the ship could remain afloat, even

DISASTER AT A GLANCE
WHAT: The luxury liner, *Titanic*, strikes an iceberg and sinks
WHERE: The Atlantic Ocean
WHEN: April 14–15, 1912
WHY: Messages reporting icebergs drifting ahead were ignored.
DEATHS: 1,517
AFTERMATH: The universal distress call, "SOS," was developed. Stricter regulations concerning sufficient lifeboats were enacted.

© Mark Twain Media, Inc., Publishers

if four compartments were to become filled with water. And, as a further guarantee of its buoyancy, it was equipped with a double bottom.

However, for all its luxurious accommodations and safety precautions, the *Titanic* was extremely lacking in one capacity. The great ship carried only the regulation 16 lifeboats, capable of carrying only 1,178 of the 2,223 passengers and crew members on board.

On April 10, 1912, as the *Titanic* set sail on its maiden voyage from Southhampton, England, to New York, its passengers remained cheerfully unaware of the dreadful shift their voyage would soon take. Aboard the ship that day were many distinguished passengers, including several well-known millionaires. Among the most notable were John Jacob Astor and his new bride, who were just returning from their honeymoon, mining magnate Bernard Guggenheim, and Isidor Strauss, head of Macy's department store.

The *Titanic* began its voyage quite uneventfully. However, by the fourth day, the radio operator had begun to receive several warnings from the ships ahead of it. They reported that icebergs were drifting unusually far south. Messages continued to come in throughout the day, but they were largely ignored. Captain Edward Smith, confident of the *Titanic's* sturdy construction, continued in the same direction without reducing speed.

Then, just before midnight on Sunday, April 14, 1912, a look-out suddenly cried, "Iceberg right ahead!" Thirty-seven seconds later, the ice began cutting a 300-foot gash into the ships hull. Five of the 16 watertight compartments quickly became flooded.

Although the ship was in grave danger, many passengers, having only felt a slight tremor when the iceberg was struck, refused to believe anything was wrong. On the deck, many of the passengers played with the ice from the iceberg, kicking it around and having snowball fights with it. Even as the stewards were going from room to room, advising passengers to evacuate their cabins and prepare to board lifeboats, many first-class passengers chose to remain inside where it was warm, still believing the *Titanic* was unsinkable.

The conditions in third class were dramatically different, however. As a result of being confined to the lower decks, many passengers had already realized that something was drastically wrong. Their cabins had begun to fill rapidly with freezing water. They tried desperately to get to the boat deck where the lifeboats were, but all the entrance doors were locked. Indeed, survival was clearly a right of the privileged. Women and children in first class were given top priority, while those in third class were all but forgotten.

In addition to prioritizing survivors, ship officers allowed many of the lifeboats to leave only half full. In fact, the first boat, having a capacity of 65 people, left with only 28 passengers. The lifeboats had to be lowered 75 feet from the liner's deck to the icy water. As they slowly descended, officers in the lifeboats fired their revolvers in order to discourage third-class passengers from jumping into the boats as they passed.

In the end, the value of human life seemed to be measured by wealth. Among the first-class passengers, only four of the women died, and three did so by choice, wishing to remain on the sinking ship with their husbands. In all, 199 of the 329 first-class passengers were saved, and 119 of the 285 second-class passengers were saved, while only 174 of the 710 third-class passengers were saved, and only 214 of the 899 crew members were saved. The final death toll was 1,517.

As a result of the staggering death count, the universal distress call, "SOS," was developed in order for it to be easily sent out and recognized. Also, stricter Board of Trade regulations were developed. These regulations required all ships to carry sufficient lifeboats to carry everyone on board. No longer would passengers perish because of a lack of lifeboats.

© Mark Twain Media, Inc., Publishers

Name_____ Date _____

Make Your Own Iceberg

What You'll Need:

- Food coloring (any color)
- A jar filled with tap water
- A large jar filled with hot tap water

- An ice cube tray
- Spoon for stirring

Follow these steps.

1. First add some of the food coloring to the jar of tap water. You should be sure to stir in enough of the coloring so that the water becomes a bright color.
2. Once the color is bright enough, pour it into the ice cube tray.
3. Now put the tray into a freezer overnight.
4. As soon as you are sure the water in the tray is frozen, get your jar of hot tap water ready.
5. Be sure to ask an adult for help when handling the hot water.
6. Take one of the ice cubes and place it carefully on the water's surface.

Answer the following question.

1. What happens?_____

_____

2. Does the ice cube float or sink? _____

3. Why do you suppose this is? _____

_____

_____

4. Observe the ice-cube for a few minutes. What happens as the water warms the ice cube?

_____

_____

5. Why do you suppose this is? _____

_____

_____

© Mark Twain Media, Inc., Publishers

Name _____ Date _____

You Are the Captain

Several factors contributed to the SS *Titanic's* demise. Iceberg warnings from other ships were repeatedly ignored as the ship continued to race ahead at its full speed of 22 knots. Captain Smith posted look-outs in the crow's nest, but they had no binoculars. Many passengers claimed that they saw the iceberg a full 20 minutes before the look-out did. As a result, it is believed that the look-out may have suffered from night-blindness due to a diet deficiency.

Although the warning of the iceberg came late, there was still enough time for the ship to steer clear of it. However, there was a delay in reaction in the engine room, and the lost time allowed the *Titanic* to be ripped open by the iceberg. Ironically, it is believed that if the ship had hit the iceberg head on, it would have caused little damage.

Once the damage was done, passengers refused to board the lifeboats. Of those who did want to board, men and third-class passengers were denied access to the first boats. A strict policy of "women and children first (and especially those of the first class)" was being followed by the ship's officers. As a result, most of the boats were leaving only half full.

In a final act of selfishness, of the over 1,500 people drowning and freezing in the water, only 13 were picked up by the unfilled lifeboats.

Using sources found at your local library and on the Internet, see what other mistakes were made and how they could have been avoided. Now, imagine that you were the captain of the *Titanic*. What do you think you would have done to save the *Titanic* and its passengers? Describe what you think could have been done to avoid the wreck and, presuming a wreck was unavoidable, how more lives could have been saved that night.

_____

_____

_____

_____

_____

_____

_____

_____

_____

_____

_____

_____

Name _____ Date _____

Different Rules for Different Classes

Using sources at your local library, research the different accommodations for the different classes on the *Titanic.* Now, imagine you are a member of either the first class, second class, or third class. Using the following questions as a guide, write several diary entries on your own paper describing your experiences on the *Titanic.*

1. Why are you traveling on the *Titanic?*

2. Are you returning from a vacation or perhaps emigrating to a better life in America?

3. Are you traveling with anyone, or did you board by yourself?

4. What are conditions like in your cabin?

5. What are your eating conditions?

6. What are your days like on the *Titanic?*

7. Do you have confidence in the "unsinkable" *Titanic?*

8. What are you doing when the *Titanic* hits the iceberg?

9. Are you aware of any danger?

10. When the steward tells you to put on your life jacket and go to the boat deck, are you alarmed?

11. Do you do as he says, or do you stay inside your warm room?

12. If you decide to go to the boat deck, are you able to get there?

13. Are you allowed to board a lifeboat right away?

14. If so, do you?

15. What happens to you? Do you live or die?

© Mark Twain Media, Inc., Publishers

Terror in America's Heartland

THE OKLAHOMA CITY BOMBING

The FBI defines **terrorism** as "the unlawful use of force or violence against persons or property to intimidate or coerce a government, the civilian population, or any segment thereof, in furtherance of political or social objectives." Terrorism usually results because a person or group is dissatisfied with a political or social system or policy coupled with the inability to change it using conventional means. Because terrorism generates media coverage, many individuals and groups resort to terrorist activities, such as hijackings, hostage takings, and bombings, in order to spread their message to the public.

The worst terrorist attack on U.S. soil took place on April 19, 1995. At 9:03 a.m., almost half of the nine-story Alfred Murrah Federal Building in downtown Oklahoma City was demolished when a fertilizer-and-diesel-fuel bomb located inside a rental truck, exploded. The bomb, made from ingredients readily available at farm supply stores, created an explosion so devastating, it was felt as far as 30 miles away and spread debris over a large area of downtown.

The nation watched in disbelief as bodies were pulled from the debris for almost two weeks. After the rescue and recovery operation was finished, the final count was 168 people killed and 600 more injured, including children who were attending a day care center in the building.

Investigators originally entertained two possible scenarios. They first suspected a group of Islamic fundamentalists in Oklahoma City. However, no threat was made prior to the explosion of the bomb. The second possibility was that the explosion was in retaliation for a federal siege that had taken place on a Branch Davidian compound in Waco, Texas, two years earlier. The Bureau of Alcohol, Tobacco, and Firearms, who led the siege in Waco, was located in the Murrah Building. Also, the explosion came on the second anniversary of the siege.

As investigations into the bombing continued, the names of two individuals, believed to be members of an organized extremist group, began to emerge. Timothy McVeigh and Terry Nichols, who had established a close bond while in the army together, soon became the primary suspects in the investigation and were immediately placed under arrest.

Timothy McVeigh was found guilty on 11 counts in the bombing, including the use of a weapon of mass destruction that caused death and injury and the use of a weapon of mass destruction to kill people and destroy federal property. He was sentenced to death. Terry Nichols was found guilty of conspiracy and manslaughter in the bombing, but was found not guilty of premeditated murder. Terry Nichols was sentenced to life in prison without parole for his role in the bombing. These were the sentences in the federal trials. As this is written, both men still may face charges in Oklahoma where the crime occurred.

Eventually, the remainder of the Murrah Building was imploded. But, even with this symbol of the pain and anger caused by terrorism gone, Americans will never be the same. Buildings can never be made bombproof. Any illusion of safety Americans felt prior to the bombing is gone. This type of terrorism has happened before, and with growing political unrest, it is likely to happen again. Unfortunately, the success of the Murrah building bombing may encourage imitators.

DISASTER AT A GLANCE

WHAT: A terrorist bombs the nine-story Alfred Murrah Federal Building

WHERE: Downtown Oklahoma City

WHEN: April 19, 1995

WHY: Reportedly, McVeigh was angry with the government because of the seige of the Branch Davidian compound in Waco, Texas.

COST: It is estimated that the cost will be more than $1 billion.

DEATHS: 168 killed, 600 injured

AFTERMATH: The Murrah Building was razed. Timothy McVeigh and Terry Nichols were both convicted of the crime.

Name_____ Date _____

Oklahoma City Quiz

Complete the following statements using information from the narritive on the Oklahoma City bombing.

1. The worst terrorist attack on U.S. soil took place on_____.

2. Almost half of the nine-story_____ in Oklahoma City was demolished.

3. The bomb was located inside a _____.

4. _____ people were killed and _____ more were injured.

5. Officials first thought the bombing was the work of a group of_____ fundamentalists.

6. They also thought the bomb may have been retaliation for the federal siege on a Branch Davidian compound in_____, Texas.

7. The siege was led by The Bureau of _____, _____, and _____ .

8. The explosion came on the_____ anniversary of the siege.

9. _____ and _____ were arrested and convicted of the bombing.

10. The two had become close in the_____.

11. _____ was found guilty on 11 counts in the bombing.

12. _____ was found guilty of conspiracy and manslaughter.

13. The remainder of the Murrah building was _____.

14. The success of the bombing could encourage _____.

© Mark Twain Media, Inc., Publishers

Name _____ Date _____

Research and Thinking on Terrorism

People have many different views when it comes to terrorism. Using sources at your local library and on the Internet, research the following questions and form your own opinions.

1. What is terrorism? _____

_____

_____

2. What causes terrorism? _____

_____

_____

3. What are some of the motives for terrorism? _____

_____

_____

4. What role do the media play in terrorism? _____

_____

5. Do terrorists use the media to publicize their beliefs? _____

_____

6. If so, how? _____

_____

_____

7. How does terrorism affect our everyday lives? _____

_____

_____

8. What does the future hold for terrorism? _____

_____

9. Which poses a bigger threat to our society, American terrorists or foreign terrorists?

_____

10. What can the United States do to prevent terrorism in the future? _____

_____

_____

_____

A Swirling Funnel of Death

TORNADOES

A tornado, or twister, is a swiftly rotating wind that blows around in a small space of extremely low pressure. On the inside of a tornado, the air is sucked in an upward direction and begins to spin around at a tremendous speed.

These swirling funnels of air rotate in a counter-clockwise direction, picking up any dust and debris in their paths. This stray debris is what makes the tip of a tornado appear so dark and ominous.

Tornadoes are generally accompanied by severe thunderstorms, when the air is the most unstable. Cold, dry air begins to flow above the warm, humid air near the ground. The jet stream begins to carry away the air on top, and the air on the bottom is then sucked up to replace it. This results in an unstable atmosphere, because the warm air is continually rising up from the ground. This is often how thunderstorms and, ultimately, tornadoes are formed.

One of the first signs that a tornado is on the way is rotating clouds that form bulges at the base of the storm. If these clouds continue to drop, a skinny funnel will form inside the cloud, extending down towards the ground. Sometimes, numerous funnels can extend from just a single storm cloud.

Although tornadoes represent a very powerful type of storm, they are usually quite small. The funnel's diameter is only about 100 to 200 yards wide, and it travels at a speed of about 20 to 40 miles per hour. At the center of the tornado, however, winds can exceed 250 m.p.h., the fastest winds on the earth.

While tornadoes usually only last about 15 minutes, they can cause great devastation in the areas where they touch down. As a result of the extremely low pressure inside the tornado, buildings may explode as the normal pressure inside the structure pushes outward. The strong updraft in the middle of the tornado sucks up everything in its path and then hurls it back to the ground.

Amazingly, though, tornadoes have been known to suck up objects and set them down miles away, totally undisturbed. For instance, once during a tornado, a woman taking a bath was picked up in her bathtub and set down, unharmed, several miles from her home.

Tornadoes can occur in several parts of the world. However, most tend to take place in the United States in the spring and summer months. In fact, the United States averages over 700 tornadoes a year, with most striking the "tornado belt" or "tornado alley," as it is sometimes called. The tornado belt is located in the central plains states, focusing on Texas, Oklahoma, and Kansas.

Tornadoes can develop at any time of the day, but are most frequently spotted in the late afternoon, when the surface air is most unstable.

Evidence of the destructive nature of tornadoes was witnessed by many on March 18, 1925, as one of the worst tornadoes in the history of the United States ripped through the Midwestern states of Missouri, Illinois, and Indiana. Its path was three-quarters of a mile wide, and it traveled for 219 miles at approximately 60 miles per hour. Although it only lasted 18 minutes, 689 people were killed and 2,000 were injured. In addition, 15,000 people lost their homes to the destruction.

© Mark Twain Media, Inc., Publishers

Name _____ Date _____

Create Your Own Tornado

What You'll Need:

- Two one-liter plastic soda bottles
- Tap water
- Food coloring (any color)
- Masking Tape

Follow these steps.

1. Add a few drops of the food coloring to one of the soda bottles, and fill it three-fourths of the way full of water.
2. Place the bottle with the water mouth to mouth with the empty bottle.
3. Using the masking tape, seal the bottles together.
4. Turn the joined bottles over, so that the one filled with water is now on top.
5. After swirling the bottles for several seconds, place them on a table.
6. Observe what happens to the water. A whirlpool should form in the top bottle as the water drains into the bottom bottle.

Make Tornado Air Rings

What You'll Need:

- A one-gallon plastic milk jug
- A candle

Follow these steps.

1. Be sure to ask an adult for help when trying this experiment.
2. Aim the opening of the milk jug at the lit candle.
3. Slap the bottom of the jug forcefully with your hand.

Answer the following question.

1. What happens? _____

_____

_____

If the jug was aimed correctly, the air ring will have blown out the candle.

© Mark Twain Media, Inc., Publishers   112

Name _____ Date _____

Make a Bolt of Lightning

What You'll Need:

- Large, thick, plastic sheet
- Masking tape
- Modeling clay

- Metal dish
- Metal object, such as a spoon

Follow these steps.

1. Fold the plastic sheet in two, and tape it securely to the table.
2. Place the clay in the center of the dish.
3. Holding on to the clay, rub the dish vigorously across the plastic for several seconds.
4. Turn out the lights and hold the metal object close to the dish.

Answer the following questions.

1. What happens? _____

_____

_____

_____

_____

_____

2. Why do you suppose this happens? _____

_____

_____

_____

_____

_____

_____

_____

_____

Name _____ Date _____

Measure the Speed of Wind

What You'll Need:

- Index card
- Paper clip

Follow these steps.

1. Attach the paper clip to the top left-hand corner of the index card.
2. Using the diagram below as a guide, print the numbers 0 through 10 on the card.

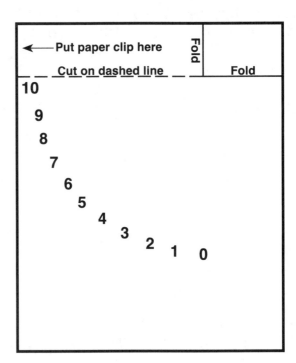

3. Cut and fold the card as indicated. This will be your wind-speed meter.
4. On the next windy day, take your wind-speed meter outside with you.
5. Hold the meter up so that it faces the wind.
6. What number does the paper clip point to on the meter? This is the wind speed in miles per hour.

© Mark Twain Media, Inc., Publishers   114

Killer Wave
Tsunami

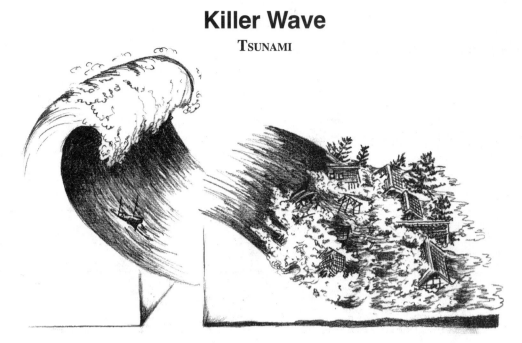

When people in the United States think about natural disasters, they generally think about flooding, hurricanes, earthquakes, or tornadoes. Almost no one worries about a **tsunami**, but they should. A tsunami, a Japanese word meaning "harbor wave," can be the most devastating natural disaster that can happen. In fact, over the past 100 years, about 75,000 people have lost their lives to these killer waves.

News reporters often use the term **tidal waves** to describe a tsunami, but this is a mistake. A tsunami has nothing to do with the tide. The tide is influenced by the gravitational pull of the moon. Tsunamis are usually caused by underwater earthquakes called **seaquakes**. Occasionally they can be triggered by coastal earthquakes on the land or by volcanic action, but the most devastating tsunamis are the ones caused by seaquakes.

Tsunamis are among the most terrifying natural hazards known to man, since they happen quickly, often without warning. The energy released in a seaquake creates waves that travel along the ocean floor at speeds of up to 500 miles an hour and may be over 100 feet high. As the tsunami enters the shallow water near the coast, it slows down, but gets taller, creating a gigantic wave. This massive wall of water has the potential to destroy entire villages and kill everything in its path. Those not killed by the force of the wave are often drowned in the deluge of water.

Most tsunamis have occurred in the islands and countries that border the Pacific Ocean. However, that does not mean that other countries should not be concerned about this type of disaster. The mainland United States, Alaska, and Hawaii have also experienced tsunamis. The discovery of an underwater 600-mile-long fault off the Pacific coast makes the United States vulnerable to tsunamis. The last big quake along this fault was 300 years ago, and by studying old, dead forests in Oregon, geologists have discovered that tsunamis occur every 300 to 400 years. When the next quake will occur, we do not know. We do know, however, that one will occur.

In order to prepare for this catastrophe, the federal government is spending about $2 million a year for a system designed to warn coastal cities. A series of warning buoys with instruments to detect underwater earthquakes are being placed in the ocean from Alaska to Chile. An early warning could spell the difference between life and death for many. If the earthquake occurs close to Japan, residents of the Pacific coast of the United States would have several hours to evacuate the area. If it happened just off the coast, however, there would be only a few minutes warning, if that.

© Mark Twain Media, Inc., Publishers   115

Name _____ Date _____

Research and Thinking on Tsunamis

After researching tsunamis in the library or on the Internet, answer the following questions.

1. What causes a tsunami? _____

_____

2. Why are tsunamis so destructive? _____

_____

_____

3. What is a seismic station? _____

_____

4. What is the International Tsunami Warning System? _____

_____

_____

5. In the open ocean, a tsunami is less than a few feet high, but its wave height increases rapidly as it encounters shallow water near the shore. Why?

_____

_____

6. What should you do if you are warned a tsunami is on its way? _____

_____

_____

_____

7. Research a specific tsunami and describe it. Give the date, location, destruction caused, and so on.

_____

_____

_____

_____

_____

_____

_____

© Mark Twain Media, Inc., Publishers   116

A Sleeping Giant Awakes
THE ERUPTION OF MOUNT SAINT HELENS

Mount Saint Helens in Washington State, just 50 miles from Portland, Oregon, was a very beautiful mountain. Its rounded top supported by an almost conical shape tower 9,677 feet high gave one the impression it had been designed by an artist. The Native Americans referred to the mountain as a beautiful and temperamental woman. The mountain was called temperamental because in the past, the volcano had erupted causing death and the loss of plant and animal life. Settlers, however, were taken by the beauty of the mountain. Many felt that the beauty of Mount Saint Helens rivaled that of Mount Fuji in Japan.

Mount Saint Helens had been dormant for 123 years. Then, suddenly, a small earthquake was detected on March 20, 1980. Soon after, following a series of earthquakes, Earth scientists began to closely watch the volcano. Believing another eruption was not far away, they began to place motion-sensitive instruments around Mount Saint Helens. These would help the scientists to monitor the movements inside the mountain.

Finally, on March 27, Mount Saint Helens erupted for the first time in over a century. By the next day, it had erupted several more times, throwing hot steam and ash three kilometers into the air. Mount Saint Helens continued to erupt for several days, creating a second crater on its top. The flames and volcanic gases bounced from one crater to the other, melting the ice and snow covering the mountain top. As a result, dangerous mudslides rushing down the sides of the mountain gave residents another reason for concern. Fearing for their safety, many evacuated.

Even as residents were leaving, tourists, news reporters, and photographers were arriving. Many flew over the active volcano and still others hiked their way to the top to get a glimpse inside. The exploding volcano offered an awesome show, and selling souvenir items became quite a lucrative business.

By April and May, however, the volcano had become extremely dangerous. Scientists warned a violent eruption was about to take place. On May 18 at 8:32 a.m., it did. The force of the eruption has been compared to 10 million tons of dynamite or the largest hydrogen bomb ever exploded.

All the people and wildlife in the area were instantly killed. In addition to the lives lost that day, hundreds of residents were left homeless. Roads, highways, and railways were destroyed. Volcanic rock and ash filled rivers and streams. Entire forests were leveled. High winds spread much of the ash across Washington and Oregon, burying the land under 10 centimeters of debris.

In the end, Mount Saint Helens killed 60 people, destroyed hundreds of millions of dollars' worth of land and property, and resulted in millions of dollars of clean-up costs. It was the most destructive volcanic eruption in the history of the United States.

In addition to the loss of life and the tremendous cost in terms of property and clean-up, the beautiful mountain lost much of her beauty. The explosion blew away about a cubic mile of the mountain and left a huge crater. Today it is 8,300 feet high. Almost 1,400 feet lower than it was before the explosion.

In 1982, Mount Saint Helens and its surrounding area were dedicated as the Mount Saint Helens National Volcanic Monument in an effort to educate visitors about the astonishing power of this volcano, whose eruption took an entire country by surprise.

DISASTER AT A GLANCE

WHAT: Mount Saint Helens, a volcano, erupts. It was the most destructive volcanic eruption in the history of the United States.

WHERE: In the state of Washington

WHEN: May 18, 1980

WHY: The eruption was triggered by a series of earthquakes that began on March 20.

DEATHS: Sixty people died. Hundreds of millions of dollars' worth of land and property were destroyed.

Name _____ Date _____

Volcanoes Vocabulary

How well do you understand the following terms dealing with volcanoes? Below and to the left are a number of definitions. In the blank after each definition, write the word that is described by the definition. The words that define the terms are given below.

Definition	**Term**
1. Rocks, ashes, and lava form this kind of volcano.	_____
2. The layer of air surrounding the earth	_____
3. After lava cools and hardens, this kind of rock is formed.	_____
4. The central tube of a volcano, which transfers magma to the earth's surface	_____
5. The hot, melted rock located deep within the earth	_____
6. The bowl-shaped depression located at the opening of the volcano	_____
7. An erupting volcano	_____
8. The earth's outermost layer of rock	_____
9. What happens when an active volcano emits materials such as ash, gas, and lava	_____
10. Scientists who study volcanoes	_____
11. A deep crack in the earth's crust	_____
12. The characteristic rock takes on when it is liquefied by intense heat	_____
13. A volcano that is no longer active	_____
14. A glassy, black rock formed by volcanic materials	_____
15. Small pieces of volcanic rock that are often released during an explosion	_____
16. A large mass of the earth's crust	_____
17. A volcano that is "sleeping," but still capable of erupting at any time	_____
18. An instrument that records the location, duration, and strength of an earthquake	_____
19. The hot, melted rock that pours out of a volcano	_____
20. An instrument used by scientists to determine the magnitude of the swell of a volcano	_____

active, ash, atmosphere, basalt, chimney, composite, crater, crust, dormant, eruption, extinct, fissure, lava, magma, molten, obsidian, plate, seismograph, tiltmeter, volcanologists

A Gentle Neighbor Turns Deadly
Mount Vesuvius

Probably the most famous volcanic eruption in history is the eruption of Mount Vesuvius near the Roman town of Pompeii on August 24, A.D. 79. Three thousand years had passed since the last eruption of Mount Vesuvius, and the Romans, believing the volcano to be extinct, had finally finished rebuilding Pompeii after an earthquake had destroyed it $17\frac{1}{2}$ years earlier.

On August 23, the Romans had celebrated a holiday marked by a feast to Vulcan, the god of subterranean fire. On August 24, the Romans were to begin celebrating a national holiday, planned to last several days.

Although the courthouse was closed due to the holiday, the day started much like any other. Business went on as usual as vendors set out their goods in the streets and merchants opened shop. However, a few strange events had occurred in previous days. Wells of water suddenly went dry. Cattle grazing on the slopes of the mountain howled. Also, Marcus Herennius, a Pompeiian politician, was rumored to have been struck dead by a firebolt that snapped out of a cloudless sky. Even so, most citizens continued to live their lives as usual.

By one o'clock, however, a huge, threatening cloud had developed over Mount Vesuvius. Residents of Pompeii gathered in the streets to peer into the sky, curious about the cause of the strange darkness. As they stood in the streets, volcanic bombs with a diameter of a foot or more rained down on them. Lightning began to flash in the ominous cloud, and a shower of ash and pale gray stones began to fall. As a result of the falling debris, the Sun was completely blocked, leaving the city in darkness for three days.

During this time, many residents tried to escape, while others decided to stay inside, hoping the danger would soon pass. In the end, the city of Pompeii, along with at least 2,000 of its citizens, was buried by 15 to 25 feet of ash and pumice.

The town of Herculaneum, a seaside resort just west of Mount Vesuvius, ended quite differently. At first, most of the debris was carried south toward Pompeii, leading many to believe Herculaneum would be spared. Still, as soon as the eruptions began, many residents began to flee toward Naples.

Although Herculaneum managed to escape most of the ash-fall, a new danger threatened the town's existence. Soon after the main eruption had ceased, an intense rainfall began, turning the ash on the upper slopes of the volcano into mud. Herculaneum was quickly buried under 65 feet of the mud. Since most of the residents had already evacuated, however, there were few casualties.

The cities of Pompeii and Herculaneum remained buried under debris for more than 1,700 years. In fact, those who lived in the area even forgot the name of Pompeii and forgot where it was located. However, sealed in a tomb of mud, dust, and debris, Pompeii and Herculaneum were time capsules preserving life as it was nearly 2,000 years ago.

When they were finally unearthed in 1860, the towns offered a clear-cut history of the lives of their residents. Although the bodies of the victims had decomposed long ago, they left imprints in the ash that were completely intact. Archeologist Guiseppi Fiorelle immediately began to pour plaster of Paris into these perfectly preserved molds. As a result, plaster casts of the victims have provided historians with a valuable glimpse into the lives of the citizens prior to their deaths.

DISASTER AT A GLANCE

WHAT: Mount Vesuvius, an Italian volcano, erupts.

WHERE: Pompeii, a Southern Italian town

WHEN: August 24, A.D. 79

DEATHS: At least 2,000 people died.

AFTERMATH: Pompeii, Herculaneum, and many of their citizens were covered for more than 1,700 years. Excavation began in 1860, revealing much about Roman life in this period.

Name _____ Date _____

Build Your Own Volcano

What You'll Need:

- Red food coloring
- Vinegar
- Small plastic bottle
- Funnel

- Sodium bicarbonate
- Large tray
- Sand
- Gravel

Follow these steps.

1. Add several drops of red food coloring to the vinegar, until it becomes a bright red.
2. Using the funnel to guide you, fill the bottle half full of sodium bicarbonate.
3. Place the bottle in the center of the tray in an upright position.
4. Place first the gravel, then the sand, around the bottle, building a volcano.
5. When you have a sufficient volcano, begin pouring the vinegar into its "mouth."

1.

2.

3.–5.

Answer the following questions.

1. What happens?_____

_____

_____

_____

2. Why do you suppose this happens?_____

_____

_____

_____

_____

© Mark Twain Media, Inc., Publishers

Name _____ Date _____

Build an Underwater Volcano

What You'll Need:

- Small bottle with a narrow neck
- Large glass jar with a wide mouth
- String
- Cold water
- Hot water
- Red food coloring

Follow these steps.

1. Tie one end of a long piece of string around the neck of the bottle. Make sure the string is tied securely.
2. Now, tie the other end of the string around the neck of the same bottle, forming a large loop.
3. Fill the large glass jar three-fourths of the way full with cold water.
4. Fill the small bottle with hot water. Add several drops of food coloring to the hot water, until it becomes a bright red.
5. Now, holding the bottle by the loop of string, carefully lower it into the jar of cold water.

Answer the following questions.

1. What happens?_____

_____

_____

_____

2. Why do you suppose this happens?_____

_____

_____

_____

_____

_____

Possible Future Disasters

You have read about and studied famous disasters throughout history, but what about the future? What possible disasters do we have to worry about? Should we just be concerned with the kinds of disasters that humans have always experienced, or should we consider other disasters that might be even more catastrophic? Could one of these future disasters be so enormous that it might eliminate or alter life on earth? Here are some potential disasters scientists and others have listed as possible dangers to humans and the planet in the years to come.

Pollution. Pollution occurs when materials are added to the environment that contaminate or spoil the environment. When people talk about pollution, they are usually referring to water pollution and air pollution. Clean water and air is essential for life. Without them, plants, animals, and humans cannot exist. Increasingly, both are becoming more polluted. Chemical wastes, garbage, and oil spills contaminate the water. Water that falls in the form of rain used to be pure, but it is not always that way today because the air is no longer clean. Gases and other pollutants from factories combine with the rain to make acid rain that destroys forests. When the forests are gone, the creatures that lived in them are also lost. When acid rain finds its way to rivers and lakes, the fish and plants that inhabit them may die.

Deforestation. When we talk about clearing land and cutting down trees, we usually hear the term "rain forests." Actually, deforestation is destroying any forest or wooded area. Deforestation occurs as populations clear land to raise livestock and crops for a growing population. It has been estimated that, in the last 30 years, 20 percent of all forests have been lost. Millions of acres are lost each year.

We should be concerned that our forests are disappearing because they play an important role in our ecosystem. They provide shade to keep temperatures cool, maintain moisture, and prevent soil runoff. Trees also remove carbon dioxide, ozone, and nitrous oxide from the air. When the trees are burned, the carbon that is in their leaves, branches, and trunks is released in the form of carbon dioxide. Burning trees and forests contributes to global warming.

Global Warming. Many scientist believe the world is becoming warmer because of a phenomenon called the **greenhouse effect**. A greenhouse is a building made of glass or plastic that enables plants to grow in cold weather. The rays of the Sun warm the air and soil inside the greenhouse. This warmth is trapped by the greenhouse and provides an environment for plants to thrive, even though it may be cold outside. The earth is like a greenhouse. The rays of the Sun warm the air and soil on Earth. The warmth is trapped by the gasses surrounding the earth and provides an environment for plants, animals, and humans to thrive in, even though space, which surrounds the earth, is very cold.

It is important that there is just the right amount of gases surrounding the earth in order for the environment and humans to survive. If there were not enough gas, too much heat would escape, and the earth would be too cold for life to exist. If there were too much gas, too little heat would escape, and the earth would be too hot for life to exist. This may be what is happening now.

© Mark Twain Media, Inc., Publishers

Many scientists believe that humans are sending so much carbon dioxide into the atmosphere that the earth is gradually warming up. Smoke from cars, factories, and forest fires all contribute to this problem. Methane gas from coal mines, landfills, cows, and other farm animals add to the problem. Another contributing factor are the CFCs released from air conditioners, aerosol sprays, and other products.

What are the consequences of global warming? Rising temperatures would make hot summers hotter, and there would be less precipitation. Winters would not be so cold. The Midwest, now known as the wheat belt, would no longer be able to produce wheat. It would be too hot and too dry. Canada, Russia, and other countries in the north, that are now considered too cold for farming, would be able to produce food.

Perhaps the biggest change would be in the sea level. Warmer temperatures would melt many glaciers and some of the polar ice caps. Some scientists have reported that this may be beginning to occur. Antarctica, the fifth largest continent, is almost completely covered with ice, yet recent photographs reveal that glaciers appear to be melting in this area. If this continues, the results could be disastrous. Coastlines and low-lying areas would be covered by water. The oceans would be larger, and the land would become smaller.

Comet Disaster. Could a huge comet or asteroid slam into Earth, causing a worldwide disaster? It is certainly possible. About every century, a large comet passes close to the earth, and

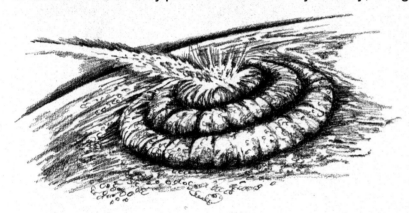

there is evidence that some have slammed into our planet. You may have read that many scientists believe that an asteroid colliding with the earth is what destroyed the dinosaurs 65 million years ago. They estimate that an asteroid 6–10 miles across collided with Earth, and the impact was so great it sent waves of vaporized fireballs of rock skimming the earth. The resulting fire, smoke, dust, and vaporized rock blocked out the Sun for several months, destroying most of the life on the planet.

More recently, a meteorite crashed to Earth in Siberia in 1908. How big the meteorite was is unknown, but the impact was tremendous. It destroyed the forest in which it landed. Seismographs recorded the impact as far away as Germany, Washington, and Java. Since the meteorite landed in one of the most remote areas on earth, little attention was paid to it. But consider what would have happened if it had landed on a major city. It is likely that millions of people would have been killed. If it had landed in the ocean, giant tsunamis would have been created, swamping coastlines and killing countless people. If it had landed on one of the poles, ice would have been melted, causing changes in the sea level as well as climatic changes.

Ozone Depletion. Several miles above the earth in the **stratosphere** is a layer of **ozone** gas that protects the earth and its inhabitants from the ultraviolet rays of the Sun. **Ultraviolet rays**, called UV rays, can cause skin cancer in humans and can also harm or kill animals. UV rays have another disastrous effect. They destroy plankton, a food for many fish and other organisms. This may not seem too serious, but by destroying the food source of fish and other creatures, the food chain is broken, and the effects can be far reaching. The fish that feed off plankton die because there is nothing to eat. Then the creatures that feed off fish also die and so on up the ladder. There are other effects, as well. Large amounts of UV rays prevent seeds from growing and plants from flowering and producing seeds. Without plants, animals and humans could not exist. It is not an overstatement to say that the ozone layer is what makes life as we know it possible on earth.

Scientists tell us that the protective ozone layer has become thinner and that a hole has developed in the ozone layer over the Antarctic. The hole varies in size and may disappear, but then reappears again in the spring. After a great deal of research, scientists discovered that the ozone layer was being destroyed by **chlorofluorocarbons**. CFCs, as they are called, are chemicals used in air conditioners, aerosol sprays, some cleaning fluids, some plastic foam used in fast-food containers and packaging, and fire extinguishers. The CFCs eventually make their way from these sources to the ozone layer and destroy the ozone. Many laws have been passed to limit or eliminate the use of CFCs, but not all nations have banned their use.

Terrorism. Terrorism is a fact of modern life. Fanatics sometimes attack people or nations they perceive as their enemies. With today's technology, it takes only a small number of people to inflict harm on many. Explosives can kill hundreds of people. Biological or germ weapons cannot only cause death to thousands, it can affect future generations.

An example of terrorism occurred at the conclusion of Operation Desert Storm during the Persian Gulf War. Retreating Iraqi soldiers set fire to hundreds of oil wells. The fires shot flames up to 100 feet in the air and belched soot and smoke that turned the day into night and the night into an eerie orange glow. The temperature near the oil wells reached over 3,000°. It took several months to extinguish the wells.

Some of the wells the Iraqis tried to blow up did not burn. Instead, huge amounts of oil spilled on the ground, forming huge lakes of oil. Some of the oil remained in a pool on the surface, but some seeped below the ground, killing plants and insects. In addition, the Iraqi soldiers opened the valves on several pipelines and turned on the pumps of five Kuwaiti tankers, releasing millions of gallons of oil into the Persian Gulf. The oilslick that resulted was one of the largest in history.

Biological Disaster. Disease has always posed a threat to humans. There was a time when there were few effective treatments for illnesses such as pneumonia or tuberculosis. People tend to forget that the discovery of antibiotics and other effective drugs to treat these and other ailments have been fairly recent events. It has only been for about 60 years that antibiotics have controlled many life-threatening diseases, reduced illness and death, and increased our life expectancy.

Doctors have recently discovered some disturbing facts. Some bacteria are becoming resistant to the medicines that once killed them. As resistance to medicines grows and the development of new medicines slows, the potential for widespread uncontrolled epidemics is increased.

A related biological concern is the rise of new or recently-discovered diseases for which there are no cures. **HIV** or **AIDS** is a disease that was unknown before 1981, and it has now spread worldwide. **Ebola** is a horrible disease that has killed hundreds of people in Africa. Although it has not attacked humans in the United States, strains of the disease have been found in monkeys in several locations in the United States.

Technological Disasters. One of the ways humans have been so successful in making their lives happier and easier is through technological advances. Primitive humans spent most of their time looking for food and shelter and protecting themselves from enemies. Science and technology have enabled humans to have a steady and safe food supply, as well as comfortable homes, and most people in developed countries feel reasonably safe. However, the very technology that has made life easy for humans can produce problems and disasters.

Here are some examples of recent technological disasters:

- A thick fog of chemicals used to produce pesticides escaped from a Union Carbide plant in Bhopal, India, in December, 1984 and settled on the town and countryside. By the next day, thousands of people were dead and many more were violently ill. The exact number of those killed is unknown, but some estimate that it may be as many as 10,000. Approximately 200,000 have been injured, and tens of thousands are still receiving treatment for problems associated with the accident.
- Donora, Pennsylvania, experienced a toxic fog in 1948. Twenty people died and about 40 percent of the residents became seriously ill before the community discovered the problem was caused by poisonous gases and chemicals coming from factory smoke.
- Times Beach, Missouri, was made uninhabitable in the 1980s because the community had been soaked with dioxin, a toxin and a cancer-causing agent. The dioxin was in oil and other industrial waste that was used to spray roads and other areas to keep dust down. Numerous health problems caused by the dioxin encouraged the federal government to buy all of the homes and move the people out.
- A similar problem occurred in Love Canal, New York, in the 1970s. Over a period of several years, a chemical plant dumped thousands of containers of toxic chemicals in an abandoned canal. The chemicals eventually seeped into homes, yards, and basements, and the residents became sick. There were many birth defects, cancers, and miscarriages. This tragedy sparked other investigations of chemical dumping, and several sites around the nation were found to be contaminated by industry.

Checking What You Have Read

Use the information on possible future disasters to answer the following questions.

1. Name the gas that contributes most to the greenhouse effect. _____

2. What greenhouse gas comes from rotting garbage? _____

3. What is the name given to cutting trees in the forest or woods? _____

4. Where did a meteor slam into the earth in 1908? _____

5. How did people in Washington become aware of the meteor? _____

_____

6. What is the layer of gas that protects Earth from UV rays? _____

7. Name three things that might happen if the earth gets warmer. _____

_____

_____

8. UV is an abbreviation for what word? _____

9. How often does a comet pass close to the earth? _____

10. How large was the asteroid that destroyed the dinosaurs? _____

11. What health problem do UV rays cause in humans? _____

12. Name the organism fish eat that is killed by UV rays. _____

13. CFCs are an abbreviation for what word? _____

14. Name three products that use CFCs. _____

_____

_____

15. Antibiotics have only been around for about how many years? _____

16. What discovery concerning bacteria has doctors worried? _____

_____

17. What well-known disease was discovered in 1981? _____

18. Ebola has killed hundreds of people on which continent? _____

19. In what animal has the Ebola virus been found in the United States? _____

20. Where was the Union Carbide plant that leaked a gas killing thousands? _____

_____

21. What killed 20 people in Donara, Pennsylvania, in 1948? _____

22. What chemical was sprayed in Times Beach, Missouri, that made people so sick? _____

23. Why was it sprayed? _____

_____

24. What town in New York in the 1970s had chemicals seep into their homes? _____

_____

25. What was the name of the war in which Iraq invaded Kuwait? _____

_____

© Mark Twain Media, Inc., Publishers

Name _____ Date _____

26. What did the retreating Iraqi soldiers do to the oil wells?

_____

_____

27. When people talk about pollution, what two elements are they usually referring to?

_____

_____

28. What is the name given to rain that has been polluted with gases?

_____

29. What is released from trees when they are burned?

_____

30. Name three things humans do to increase global warming.

_____

_____

_____

31. Why do many countries cut down their forests?

_____

_____

_____

32. What percentage of all forests has been cut down in the last 30 years?

_____

33. Name three benefits of forests.

_____

_____

_____

34. What is the term scientists use to explain global warming?

_____

Name _____ Date _____

Create a Disaster Scenario

The word *scenario* is used often today, but most people do not know what it really means. A scenario is an outline of a screenplay. In this exercise you will write a scenario of an *original* disaster film. You may choose any disaster or potential disaster for your topic. The only restriction is, IT MUST BE ORIGINAL! DO NOT COPY THE PLOT OR CHARACTERS YOU HAVE SEEN IN A MOVIE OR TELEVISION SHOW! This may be tough, since so many disaster films have been written, but your scenario will be much more interesting and fun to write if it is completely original. Remember, you are not to write the screenplay, but only the scenario. All you have to do is answer the following questions in order to compete this assignment.

1. Title of Screenplay: _____

2. Main Characters. Give their names, descriptions, and relationships to one another:

_____

_____

_____

_____

_____

3. Summarize or outline the plot in one paragraph. In other words, what happens first, what else occurs, and then how does it end:

_____

_____

_____

_____

_____

_____

_____

_____

_____

_____

_____

4. Now on your own paper, write one scene from your screenplay:

   a. Describe the setting.
   b. Name and describe characters in the scene.
   c. Write the dialogue and action for the scene.

© Mark Twain Media, Inc., Publishers

Answer Keys

Disaster Crossword Puzzle (pages 2–3)

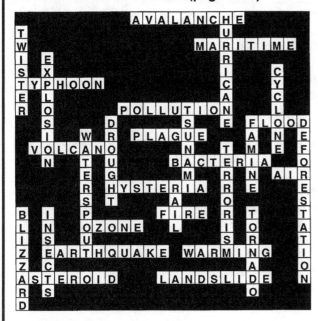

TWA Flight 800 Quiz (page 21)
1. Paris
2. Atlantic Ocean
3. 230
4. Long Island
5. French
6. Kennedy
7. three
8. Calverton
9. FBI's
10. sky
11. cockpit
12. streak of light
13. high
14. 16-month

Avalanche and Landslides Vocabulary (page 24)
1. slump
2. penetrates
3. volcano
4. terrace
5. avalanche
6. wet snow avalanche
7. rockfalls
8. rockslides
9. gravity
10. Andes
11. Alps
12. tsunami
13. landslide
14. vibration
15. erosion
16. saturated
17. slab avalanche

18. Rocky Mountains
19. dry snow avalanche
20. mudflows
21. Himalayas
22. resort
23. blasting
24. airborne powder avalanche
25. seep
26. Appalachian Mountains
27. earthquake
28. debris

Blizzard Vocabulary (page 26)
1. blizzard
2. whiteout
3. severe
4. satellite
5. radar
6. snow fence
7. meteorologist
8. forecast
9. precipitation
10. moisture
11. hypothermia
12. hazardous
13. avalanche
14. National Weather Service
15. frostbite
16. gangrene
17. accumulate
18. carbon monoxide
19. flooding
20. snow
21. windchill
22. supplementary
23. stroke
24. hearth attack
25. snowstorm
26. reservoir

Check Your Knowledge of the Blizzard of 1888 (page 28)
1. elevated trains
2. engineer
3. iron horse
4. street car
5. March 12, 1888
6. transportation
7. snow drifts
8. derailed
9. ice
10. ladders
11. 15,000
12. Tunnels
13. telephone, telegraph

© Mark Twain Media, Inc., Publishers

14. gas, water
15. week
16. $20 million
17. subway
18. burying
19. 400
20. 200
21. 100
22. populated
23. 50
24. eastern
25. 20, 26

Surviving a Blizzard (page 29)

1. What should I do in case of a blizzard?
• Take weather warnings seriously.
• If a winter storm is expected, have plenty of food in your home.
• Stock foods that do not require either cooking or refrigeration in case of power failure.
• If you heat your home with oil, check the level of fuel. Sometimes normal delivery service of fuel is disrupted during a winter storm.
• If you have a fireplace, have a supply of dry wood handy.
• Check the batteries in your flashlight and portable radio before the storm.
• Watch your local television stations or listen to your radio for weather updates
2. If I am outdoors…
• Go inside immediately. Do not venture outside to go to the store or to another location.
• If it is dangerous for some reason to stay in the house, put on several layers of loose-fitting, warm clothing and wear a hat or a hooded jacket. Cover your face with a scarf and wear heavy socks, warm winter boots, gloves, and mittens. But remember, it is almost always better to stay indoors during a blizzard.
3. If I am indoors…
• Watch your local television stations or listen to your radio for weather updates.
• If you are using a supplementary heating system, continually check it to make sure it is working properly.
4. If I am in a car…
• Before the winter season, make sure your car is ready for snowy and icy weather. Check your oil and antifreeze. Make sure the heater, brakes, and windshield wipers are in good working order.
• Keep an emergency kit in your car with the following items: warm clothing, blankets or sleeping bags, nonperishable food items and jugs of water, a flashlight with extra batteries, matches, an ice scraper, jumper cable, chains, and a shovel.
• Keep your fuel tank filled. Never drive with your fuel gauge on empty.
• If you are stranded, stay in your car and wait for help to arrive.

• If you become stranded, be careful how you use your heater. Make sure you provide plenty of ventilation. Be sure your exhaust pipe is not covered with snow.
• If you are stranded at night, keep the inside light on in your vehicle to attract help. Turning on a blinker will also attract attention.
• Keep awake in cold temperatures and move your arms and legs frequently to keep circulation going.
5. After a blizzard…
• Make sure you are dressed warmly.
• Come in often to warm up.
• Be careful building snow tunnels and forts. They can collapse and cause serious injuries.

Chernobyl Vocabulary (page 38)

1. Geiger counter
2. nuclear energy
3. nuclear fission
4. leukemia
5. atomic energy
6. sarcophagus
7. meltdown
8. cesium-137
9. radiation
10. nuclear fusion
11. nuclear reactor
12. uranium-235
13. China syndrome
14. radiation sickness
15. core
16. nucleus

Extinguish a Fire (page 39)

When baking soda and vinegar are mixed, a chemical reaction occurs. As a result, carbon dioxide is formed. Since the carbon dioxide is heavier than air, it displaces the oxygen needed for the flame to continue burning. Therefore, the flame is smothered by the non-combustible carbon dioxide. Most fire extinguishers work on this same principle. In fact, the bubbles that are sprayed out are full of carbon dioxide, which works to surround the fire and block all sources of oxygen. This was one of the many methods used to extinguish the flames caused by the 1986 chemical explosion at Chernobyl.

Check Your Knowledge of Ireland and the Famine (page 42)

1. coffin ship
2. potato
3. laissez-faire
4. lumper, spud
5. *Phytophthora infestans*
6. blight
7. tumbling
8. St. Patrick
9. pagan

© Mark Twain Media, Inc., Publishers

10. leprechaun
11. blarney stone
12. St. Patrick's Day
13. shamrock
14. green
15. west
16. King Henry VIII
17. potatoes
18. Spanish
19. South America
20. Irish Sea
21. landlords
22. four
23. peasant
24. famine

Research and Thinking for the Dust Bowl (page 45)
1. Texas and Oklahoma, and parts of Kansas, Colorado, and Nebraska.
2. Texas, Oklahoma, Kansas, Colorado, Nebraska, New Mexico, Montana, North Dakota, South Dakota, Missouri, Iowa, Arkansas, Wyoming.
3. Answers will vary.
4. Answers will vary.

Dust Bowl Vocabulary (pages 46–47)
1. agronomist
2. contour plowing
3. ecosystem
4. sod
5. terracing
6. equilibrium
7. species
8. panhandle
9. semi-arid
10. dust pneumonia
11. shelter belt
12. herbivore
13. Okie
14. drought
15. respiratory
16. nomadic
17. perennial
18. environment
19. Great Depression
20. migrant worker
21. annual
22. erode
23. carnivore
24. diversify
25. corporate farm
26. marine deposits
27. Native Americans
28. ecologist
29. organism
30. scavenger
31. reservation

32. decompose
33. graze
34. ecology
35. harvest
36. mechanization
37. black blizzard
38. Dust Bowl
39. bronchial
40. crop rotation

Improving Your Vocabulary—Dust Bowl (pages 48–49)
1. B
2. A
3. D
4. A
5. B
6. D
7. D
8. B
9. A
10. A
11. C
12. A
13. D
14. B
15. B
16. C
17. D
18. B
19. A
20. C
21. C
22. D
23. B
24. C
25. A
26. D

Earthquake Vocabulary (pages 52–53)
1. crust
2. aftershock
3. avalanche
4. fault
5. magma
6. epicenter
7. San Andreas fault
8. focus
9. Ring of Fire
10. foreshocks
11. magnitude
12. continental drift
13. paleontologist
14. Richter scale
15. loot
16. seismographs
17. seismologist

18. shock waves
19. tsunami
20. conflagration
21. mantle
22. undulate
23. fossil
24. inner core
25. outer core
26. plate
27. tremor
28. geologist
29. prehistoric
30. landslide
31. meteorologist
32. earthquake

Identify The Layers of The Earth (page 53)

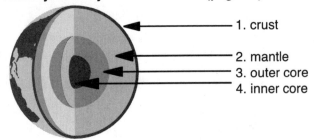

1. crust
2. mantle
3. outer core
4. inner core

Research and Thinking for Earthquakes: Mercalli Scale (page 54)

I. Not felt by people.
II. Felt indoors only by persons at rest, especially on upper floors.
III. Felt indoors by several. Hanging objects may swing slightly. Vibration like passing of light trucks.
IV. Felt indoors by many.
V. Felt indoors and outdoors by nearly everyone. Swaying of tall trees and poles sometimes noticed.
VI. Felt by all. Furniture moved or overturned. Weak plaster and masonry cracked.
VII. Difficult to stand. Damage to masonry.
VIII. Damage to weak structures. Branches broken from trees.
IX. Buildings collapse. Underground pipes broken.
X. Most masonry and frame structures destroyed. Some bridges destroyed. Serious damage to dams, dikes, embankments. Landslides on river banks.
XI. Almost all buildings and bridges destroyed. Huge fissures in ground.
XII. Damage nearly total. Waves seen on ground surfaces.

Checking What You Have Read—The New Madrid Quake (page 57)

1. New Madrid, Missouri
2. Mississippi River
3. Madrid, Spain
4. series

5. duration
6. infrastructure
7. 50 percent
8. larger
9. 90 percent
10. backwards
11. year
12. Boston, Massachusetts
13. 80 years
14. Ohio River and Natchez, Mississippi
15. December 12, 1811
16. 28
17. San Francisco, Los Angeles
18. 1895
19. sinkholes
20. Japan
21. muddy
22. sulphur
23. 8.0–8.5
24. southeast

California and the San Andreas Fault (page 60)

1. Sutter's Mill
2. Sacramento
3. San Francisco Bay
4. San Jose
5. San Francisco
6. San Andreas Fault
7. Los Angles
8. San Diego

How Are Earthquakes Measured? (page 61)

1. There are two types of seismographs. One records the horizontal movements of the earth and the other records the vertical movements of the earth. In each, a weight is attached to a spring, which is attached to the frame. When there is a tremor, the weight stays fixed, but the frame moves and a pen attached to the weight marks the movement on a paper wrapped around a cylinder that rotates.

2. The most common scale is the Richter scale, named after its inventor Charles Richter. It rates the intensity of an earthquake by taking data from a seismograph that measures the amount of energy released in the quake. The scale is from 1 to 10, with each point increase in the Richter scale meaning the earthquake is 10 times stronger than the number below. So an earthquake that measures 6 on the Richter scale is 10 times stronger than one that measures 5. The second type of scale to measure the intensity of an earthquake is called the Mercalli scale. This scale rates the intensity of an earthquake by assessing the damage it causes.

3. Many ancient people believed that earthquakes were caused by huge animals. Russians thought that a giant dog caused earthquakes when he scratched his fleas. Japanese thought they were caused by a giant catfish living in mud underground. Chinese thought the earth

was supported by eight large elephants, and when one shook its head there was an earthquake. There are several other myths in other cultures.

4. Answers will vary. Perhaps some students will suggest that animals are more sensitive or more aware of slight foreshocks that humans cannot detect.

Surviving an Earthquake (page 62)

1. What should I do to prepare in case of an earthquake?
a. Household objects, such as bookcases, cabinets, and shelves, should be secured to the walls or floor.
b. Cabinets and cupboards should be latched so the doors cannot open during a quake.
c. Breakable items and heavy items should be stored on the floor or on the lower shelves.
d. Each family member should know how to turn off the switches to the gas, electric, and water.
e. The family should develop an earthquake survival plan, discuss it, and practice it.
f. Stockpile enough canned food and drinking water for several days.
7. Store flashlight, batteries, a battery operated radio or television, fire extinguisher, and first-aid kit.

2. If I am indoors when a quake occurs, here is what I should do to survive if an earthquake occurs.
a. Stay calm.
b. Hide under a table. If no table is available, stand in a doorway.
c. Stay away from windows, chimneys, tall, heavy furniture, or anything that might topple over on you.
d. Cover your head with your arms.
e. If you are inside a public building, stay there, but stand in a doorway.
f. Be aware that there will be aftershocks.

3. If I am outdoors, here is what I should do to survive if an earthquake occur.
a. Find an open area away from buildings, trees, chimneys, walls, and power lines.
b. If you are in a car, pull to the side of the road and stop.
c. Stay off bridges and away from underpasses.
d. Stay inside until the quake is over.
e. Get to open ground, if possible.
f. Be aware that there will be aftershocks.

4. After a quake, here is what I should do.
a. Check yourself for injuries.
b. Check your family and neighbors for injuries.
c. Call a doctor or provide first aid, if needed.
d. Check for fires in your home.
e. Check for gas and water leaks. Shut them off, if they are damaged.
f. Check to see if your power lines are down, and if they are, stay away from them.
g. Be careful if you go outside. There may be downed power lines, and trees, buildings, and chimneys may be

unstable and may fall.
h. Leave the building.

Improving Your Vocabulary—Earthquakes (pages 63–64)

1. C
2. B
3. A
4. D
5. B
6. C
7. A
8. C
9. D
10. A
11. D
12. B
13. C
14. A
15. C
16. C
17. D
18. C
19. A
20. A
21. C
22. C
23. D

Research and Thinking for the Triangle Shirtwaist Co. Fire (page 68)

1. Answers will vary.
2. Answers will vary. Some will say they weren't found guilty because the victims were poor, uneducated and immigrants. The owners were rich and powerful. There are other answers as well.
3. Here is a partial list of fires that have encouraged fire safety and legislation:
Iroquois Theater, Chicago—1903; Lakeview Grammar School, Cleveland—1908; Triangle Shirtwaist Co. Fire, New York City—1911; Consolidated School, New London, Texas—1937; Coconut Grove Night Club, Boston—1942; Hotel Winecoff, Atlanta—1946; Our Lady of the Angels School, Chicago—1958; Beverly Hills Supper Club, Southgate, Kentucky—1977; MGM Grand Hotel, Las Vegas—1980; Keansburg Rest Home, Morganville, New Jersey—1981; Happy Land Social Club, New York City—1990.
4. Answers will vary.

Flood Vocabulary (page 70)

1. Nile
2. marine
3. silt
4. ocean
5. delta

6. river

7. transportation

8. flooding

9. fertile

10. lake

11. riverbed

12. flood plain

13. spillway

14. levee

15. dam

16. outlet

17. flash flood

18. irrigate

19. reservoir

20. Mississippi

21. basin

22. tsunami

23. buffer

24. inland

25. coastline

26. hurricane

Checking What You Have Read—The Raging Mississippi (page 73)

1. Hernando de Soto

2. Spain or Europe

3. gold

4. 1539

5. levee

6. bluffs

7. Mississippi

8. Gulf of Mexico

9. Rocky, Allegheny

10. big river

11. tributary

12. breach

13. Mount Landing, Arkansas

14. rain, snow

15. Arkansas, Louisiana, Mississippi

16. 300

17. 300 million dollars

18. 500,000

19. The Flood Control Act in 1928

20. 325 million

21. U.S. Army Corps of Engineers

22. nine

23. Ohio

24. tributary

25. Lake Pontchartrain

How Well Do You Know the Mississippi? (page 76)

1. 2,348

2. 100 feet

3. nine feet

4. Itasca, Minnesota

5. Gulf of Mexico

6. Any three of the following rivers: Illinois, Chippewa,

Black, Wisconsin, Saint Croix, Iowa, Des Moines, Rock, Missouri, Ohio, Arkansas, Red, White

7. Hernando de Soto and his men

8. Robert La Salle

9. Louis Jolliet, Jacques Marquette

10. It was part of the Louisiana Purchase in 1803.

11. Lewis and Clark

12. Mississippi is the boundary between the states of Minnesota, Iowa, Missouri, Arkansas, and Louisiana on the west, and Wisconsin, Illinois, Kentucky, Tennessee, and Mississippi on the east.

13. Answers will vary but may include: Minneapolis and Saint Paul, MN; La Crosse, WI; Dubuque, Davenport, and Keokuk, IA; Rock Island, Quincy, and Cairo, IL; Hannibal and St. Louis, MO; Memphis, TN; Helena, AR; Vicksburg and Natchez, MS; Baton Rouge and New Orleans, LA.

14. The Missouri

15. Ojibwa, Winnebago, Fox, Sauk, Choctaw, Chickasaw, Natchez, and Alabama

Famous Rivers (page 76)

Answers will vary since there is disagreement where some of the rivers actually begin.

River	Location	Mouth	Length
Nile	Africa	Mediterranean	4,132 miles
Amazon	S. America	Atlantic	3,900 miles
Yangtze	China	East China Sea	3,720 miles
Congo	Africa	Atlantic	2,900 miles
Mississippi	U.S.	Gulf of Mexico	2,348 miles

Research and Thinking for the Johnstown Flood (page 79)

1. The Allegheny Mountains, extend more than 500 miles from central Pennsylvania to central West Virginia and southwestern Virginia

2. To provide water for canals.

3. Any two of the following:

• For cheap and convenient transportation and shipping

• To connect one water way with another

• To circumvent an obstacle

• To connect with other canals

4. The first canal was a seven-mile-long canal built in Virginia in 1785.

5. Horses pulled them.

6. The Erie Canal, which linked the important Hudson-Mohawk Valley and New York City with the Great Lakes and the Midwest

7. Find the following dimensions of the Erie Canal:

• Depth: 4 feet

• Width: Forty feet wide at the surface and twenty-eight feet wide at the bottom

• Length: 363 miles long

8. Buffalo, NY, to the Hudson River

9. To celebrate Memorial Day

10. Two cars suspended by the same cable travel on railroad tracks. One goes up the mountain or incline and

© Mark Twain Media, Inc., Publishers

one goes down. The Johnstown Inclined Plane was built as a quick escape route for future floods. The Johnstown incline is the steepest incline of its type in the world.

11. In southwestern Pennsylvania, about 10 miles northeast of Johnstown.

12. The town was located in a valley that naturally flooded. A reservoir or lake was located on higher ground and the only thing that kept the reservoir from flowing to Johnstown was a poorly-maintained dam.

Black Death Vocabulary (page 82)

1. catapult
2. merchant
3. infected
4. stench
5. Mongol
6. plague
7. disease
8. incense
9. scented
10. victim
11. Messina
12. Black Sea
13. bubo
14. Caffa
15. Black Death
16. pestilence
17. bloodletting
18. nobility
19. aristocrats
20. villa
21. rodents
22. host
23. regurgitate
24. infectious disease
25. Middle Ages
26. Renaissance
27. superstition
28. myth

Hurricane Vocabulary (page 84)

1. eye
2. hurricane warning
3. storm surge
4. millibar
5. knot
6. storm tide
7. sea wall
8. typhoon
9. cyclone
10. hurricane
11. category 4
12. category 3
13. category 2
14. category 5
15. category 1
16. tropical depression
17. eye wall
18. hurricane watch
19. Saffir-Simpson scale
20. hurricane season

Three Infamous U.S. Hurricanes (page 89)

1. A
2. C
3. G
4. A
5. A
6. G
7. A
8. C
9. A
10. C
11. G
12. C
13. A
14. G
15. A
16. C
17. A
18. G
19. G
20. C
21. G
22. A
23. C
24. G
25. G
26. C
27. G
28. C
29. G
30. C
31. G
32. C
33. G
34. A
35. A

Research and Thinking for Hurricanes (page 91)

1. Inflation is the increase in the level of prices or the decline in the purchasing power of money over a period of time. For example, a three bedroom home may have cost $3,700 in 1900. A comparable home may cost $70,000 today. So, in order to compare the cost of the destruction of a hurricane in 1900 with the cost of the destruction of a hurricane today, we must take inflation into consideration.

2. Galveston was more densely populated than the Florida Keys were in 1935. On the other hand, meteorology, which is the science that deals with weather and weather conditions, was more advanced in 1969 than in 1900. Meteorologists were able to warn the residents a deadly hurricane was approaching, and citizens were

able to evacuate the area before it arrived. Also, improved communications—radio and television—made it easy for residents to keep informed about the approaching storm.

3. Agnes struck a wide area that had many buildings and was heavily populated.

4. The practice of naming hurricanes began in 1950. Tropical storms and hurricanes are given names to avoid confusion. A tropical storm is named when it reaches winds of 39 m.p.h.

5. The World Meteorological Organization selects the names for Atlantic Basin storms. The names are in English, Spanish, and French, because these are the languages spoken where these storms hit. Storm names alternate between male and female names and are listed alphabetically. There are six sets of names, which means each set of names is used again each six years.

6. Damage is not caused by wind alone. It is a combination of wind, storm surge, tornadoes, and rain, which causes flooding.

7. Because of the tremendous population growth, new homes, condominiums, and cities that have been built along the coast. Many current residents have not been through a devastating hurricane. They have been through milder storms and hurricanes and refuse to evacuate.

Death of the Dinosaurs Vocabulary (pages 94–95)

1. asteroid
2. quartz
3. starve
4. tsunami
5. herbivore
6. astronomer
7. vaporized
8. deciduous
9. iridium
10. angiosperm
11. climate
12. ecosystem
13. dinosaur
14. foliage
15. extinct
16. Cretaceous
17. asteroid collision theory
18. radiation
19. infertile
20. Hiroshima
21. carbon monoxide
22. comet
23. microscopic
24. diet
25. ultraviolet
26. chlorine
27. fossil
28. greenhouse effect

Reading a Map (page 100)

1. Cahaba Prison
2. St. Louis, Missouri
3. New Orleans, Louisiana
4. Vicksburg, Mississippi
5. Andersonville Prison
6. Helena, Arkansas
7. Memphis, Tennessee
8. Cairo, Illinois
9. Evansville, Indiana
10. Cincinnati, Ohio
11. Louisville, Kentucky

Sultana Study Question (page 100)

Most of the country was concentrating on other matters. Lee had surrendered. General Joseph E. Johnston was surrendering on the day before the disaster. Lincoln had been assassinated less than two weeks before. A new president had just been sworn in. The army did not want the accident publicized. Most of the important newspapers were published in the East, far away from the accident.

Steamboats and the Mississippi Quiz
(pages 101–102)

1. C
2. C
3. D
4. B
5. C
6. D
7. D
8. C
9. C
10. A
11. A
12. D
13. D
14. B
15. D
16. D
17. B
18. A
19. C
20. B

Make Your Own Iceberg (page 105)

When water freezes, it increases its volume by one-eleventh. As a result, the ice becomes lighter than the water, allowing it to float on the water's surface and project above it. As the ice begins to melt, it loses its increased volume. This allows it to sink to the bottom of the jar. While on the bottom, the ice starts to mix with the water and is warmed up. By doing this, it becomes less dense and moves back toward the water's surface. This is the reason icebergs present such a danger to ships.

© Mark Twain Media, Inc., Publishers

The captain and crew can only see their tips above the water and cannot be sure what lurks below the surface.

Oklahoma City Quiz (page 109)
1. April 19, 1995
2. Alfred Murrah Federal Building
3. rental truck
4. 168, 600
5. Islamic
6. Waco
7. Alcohol, Tobacco, Firearms
8. second
9. Timothy McVeigh, Terry Nichols
10. army
11. Timothy McVeigh
12. Terry Nichols
13. imploded
14. imitators or copycats

Research and Thinking on Terrorism (page 110)
Answers will vary.

Make a Bolt of Lightning (page 113)
Tornadoes are often accompanied by severe thunderstorms. The lightning in thunderstorms is really just a giant spark of static electricity. This lightning originates in storm clouds that are filled with an enormous amount of this static electricity.

Measure the Speed of Wind (page 114)
The number the paper clip points to is the speed the wind is traveling. For instance, if the paper clip points to the number five, this means that the wind is traveling at five miles per hour.

Research and Thinking on Tsunamis (page 116)
1. Sometimes called seismic sea waves, a tsunami is usually caused by an intense earthquake occurring near the ocean. Sometimes they can also be produced by volcanic eruptions and underwater avalanches or landslides.
2. Shallow water is what makes tsunamis a threat to humans and property. As the tsunami enters the water near the coast, its speed decreases but the height increases. The tall waves pound people and buildings causing damage and death.
3. A seismic station is a location with equipment that detects, monitors, and records earthquakes and communicates with other seismic stations in order to share data.
4. The ITWS utilizes and monitors data from many seismic and tidal stations and satellite communications throughout the Pacific Ocean and distributes tsunami watches and warnings to all the countries and territories of the entire Pacific Basin.
5. The wave energy of tsunamis extend from the surface to the bottom in the deepest waters. When the tsunami approaches the coastline, the wave energy is compressed into a much shorter distance, creating taller, destructive, life-threatening waves.
6.
• Make sure your entire family is aware of the warning.
• Your family should evacuate your house if you live in a tsunami hazard area. Move quickly, orderly, and calmly to a safe location.
• If you are at the beach or near the ocean and you feel an earth tremor, move immediately to higher ground. Don't wait for a tsunami warning to be announced. Move away from rivers and streams that lead to the ocean.
• The upper floors of tall, reinforced concrete hotels offer protection if there is not enough warning to move to higher ground.
7. Answers will vary.

Volcanoes Vocabulary (page 118)
1. composite
2. atmosphere
3. basalt
4. chimney
5. magma
6. crater
7. active
8. crust
9. eruption
10. volcanologists
11. fissure
12. molten
13. extinct
14. obsidian
15. ash
16. plate
17. dormant
18. seismograph
19. lava
20. tiltmeter

Build Your Own Volcano (page 120)
The mixture of sodium bicarbonate and vinegar causes bubbles of carbon dioxide gas to form that, in turn, force your volcano to erupt.

Build an Underwater Volcano (page 121)
Hot water will always rise to the surface of cold water. Therefore, your volcano appears to have erupted underwater, sending up a large plume of smoke.

Checking What You Have Read—Possible Disasters (pages 126–127)
1. carbon dioxide
2. methane
3. deforestation
4. Siberia
5. seismograph

6. ozone
7. Any three—Hotter summer, less precipitation, milder winter, fewer crops in the Midwest, more crops in the north, glaciers and polar caps would melt, sea level would raise, coastal and lowland flooding
8. ultraviolet
9. about once a century
10. 6–10 miles across
11. skin cancer
12. plankton
13. chlorofluorocarbons
14. Any three—air conditioners, aerosol sprays, some cleaning fluids, some plastic foam used in fast-food containers and packaging, and fire extinguishers
15. 60
16. bacteria resistant to antibiotics
17. AIDS or HIV
18. Africa
19. monkeys
20. Bhopal, India
21. a toxic fog
22. dioxin
23. to keep dust down
24. Love Canal
25. Operation Desert Storm or Persian Gulf War
26. burned them
27. air and water
28. acid rain
29. carbon dioxide
30. Any three—drive cars, build factories, clear forests, work in mines, create landfills, breed cows and other livestock, use products with CFCs
31. to raise livestock and crops for a growing population
32. 20 percent
33. Any three—They provide shade to keep temperatures cool, maintain moisture, and prevent soil runoff. Trees also remove carbon dioxide, ozone, and nitrous oxide from the air.
34. greenhouse effect

© Mark Twain Media, Inc., Publishers